THE CODE OF CONTENTMENT

**DEDICATE
A YEAR.**

**DISCOVER WHAT
MATTERS.**

PAUL TENHAKEN

WESTBOW
PRESS®
A DIVISION OF THOMAS NELSON
& ZONDERVAN

WestBow Press books may be ordered through booksellers or by contacting:

WestBow Press
A Division of Thomas Nelson & Zondervan
1663 Liberty Drive
Bloomington, IN 47403
www.westbowpress.com
844-714-3454

Cover and artwork by Mark Henderson, Clixable, Inc.
Content review, consulting by Pastor Michael Ten Haken

ISBN: 979-8-3850-2292-2 (sc)
ISBN: 979-8-3850-2293-9 (hc)
ISBN: 979-8-3850-2294-6 (e)

Library of Congress Control Number: 2024907195

Print information available on the last page.

WestBow Press rev. date: 5/3/2024

To those who have invested in, mentored, walked alongside, and cared for me on my own journey. You know who you are. Thank you.

To my wife and kids, thanks for always believing in me.

To my Lord, thank you for the unfailing promises of your Word that have guided me through the highs and lows of life in my pursuit of contentment. May you be honored and glorified through this book.

"And we know that in all things God works for the good of those who love him, who have been called according to his purpose" (Romans 8:28).

CONTENTS

HOW TO USE THIS BOOK

There is a lot of information out there about forming habits. Countless books, podcasts, seminars, and other materials are dedicated to helping people create positive habits. And while this book is not primarily intended to do that, my hope is that strong habits do become a side-effect as a result of steady engagement with *The Code of Contentment.*

This book will be most impactful if you can make a year-long commitment to completing it. A few minutes a week of reading, journaling, reflection, and prayer is all that is required. Sticking with that schedule week after week for one year has the potential to lead to significant revelations in your life and help reveal God's purpose for you.

Before you dive in, here's a quick overview of the core elements you will encounter each week and how to get the most out of *The Code of Contentment.*

1. **Weekly Reading:** It will be very important to find a regular time each week when you will spend time with *The Code of*

Contentment. Each week will be a different theme on work, health, purpose, or relationships.

2. **Quotable:** A quote you can reflect on to reinforce the weekly message.

3. **What does scripture say?** Take time to not just look at the scripture verses that apply to the weekly message, but open your Bible to absorb the full context of the featured verses.

4. **Take time to reflect on your notes from last week. What worked and what didn't?** You can't move forward without looking back and seeing what is working and not working in your life. Be sure to spend time reviewing your notes from the week prior, learn from them, and adjust accordingly for the week ahead. If you set a goal and didn't achieve it, don't get discouraged. The power lies in writing them down and spending intentional time thinking about them during the week.

5. **What is one goal I want to be intentional about accomplishing this week?** Think about something specific you want to accomplish in the week ahead. It could be a commitment to exercising three days in the week ahead, tackling a tough conversation you've been avoiding, or finally scheduling that night out with your spouse. Writing it down will dramatically increase your accountability to accomplishing it. In fact, according to Inc., writing down your goals can increase your chances of achieving them by 42%! Remember, it's only a week, so this should be something small but realistic to accomplish.

6. **What is one relationship I am going to focus on this week?** Write down someone you want to be intentional with in the week ahead. It could be giving a thank-you gift to your

mailman, a call to your sibling whom you haven't spoken to in months, a child who needs some extra time with you, or a business contact you need to muster up the courage to meet with. Writing it down and reflecting on it will greatly increase the chances of it happening!

7. **What is one thing I can do this week to better my physical and/or mental health?** Commit to taking care of yourself! Jot down some tangible ways you will do this, such as spending less time on your electronics, drinking more water, or setting a mileage goal for walking or running. Consider telling someone else your goal in order to help keep you accountable.

8. **What am I grateful for in my life right now?** Take time to simply reflect on what you are grateful for at the moment and the blessings God has provided you. In the hustle and bustle of life, being thankful can often get lost. The goal here is to slowly develop an attitude of gratitude. When you stop and spend dedicated time on this, you will be overwhelmed with His goodness!

9. **Spend time in prayer following the P.A.T.H. (Praise, Admit, Thank, Help).** At the end of each session, wrap up time talking to God in prayer. The P.A.T.H. acronym is a great format to help your time stay focused and structured.
   - First, **Praise** God for who He is and his presence in your life.
   - Second, **Admit** you have sinned and confess these sins to Him.
   - Third, **Thank** God for what he has done and continues to do in your life.
   - Finally, ask for **Help** in areas where you need his strength in your life.

INTRODUCTION

Con·tent·ment /kənˈtentm(ə)nt/ *noun:* a state of happiness and satisfaction.

One of the things many of us long for is a feeling of contentment in our lives. Afterall, to be content is to be happy, to be at peace, and to have calmness in our circumstances. For many years now, I have sought out contentment in different ways—career, family, material possessions, physical health, food, money, power, faith, and more. While some methods have brought more contentment for me than others, I firmly believe that true contentment is a journey and not a destination.

This book seeks to be a tool for discovering what contentment can look like in your own life. Using a core set of questions each week, you will have the opportunity to sharpen your perspectives on five key areas that, through my own experience, I've found to be critical to cracking the code of contentment—committing to your faith, setting goals, fostering relationships, maintaining good health, and practicing gratitude.

The Code of Contentment is not intended to be an end-all solution for those struggling to find peace and happiness in their life. However, my hope is that the questions asked each week, combined with honest reflection and journaling, will create a new perspective for you on how to lead a life of contentment.

I am excited that you have entered into this journey of self-discovery and reflection, and I can't wait for God to speak to you in the pages ahead.

One final and very important thing!

To ensure you get the most out of *The Code of Contentment*, please take five minutes to watch this quick video from me at <u>www. paultenhaken.com/code</u>

Now, let's go rolling.

WEEK 1

MASTERING THE WALK

Congratulations on embarking on this journey to invest in your mind, body, and spirit through *The Code of Contentment*. They say a journey of a thousand miles begins with a single step, and I hope this devotional serves as your first step toward a year dedicated to nurturing your relationships, enhancing your work, prioritizing your wellness, and growing in the Lord. Get ready for an enriching ride!

One of the most vital skills any leader can cultivate is the art of fostering effective, positive habits. I've had my fair share of habits over the years, not all of them being beneficial. Through engaging with *The Code of Contentment* in the coming year, my wish is for you to develop positive and life-changing habits centered on praying, fostering relationships, practicing gratitude, and evolving into the leader and individual who aligns with God's design for you.

Here's my personal request: *commit to this book for a year*. With fifty-two individual lessons and devotionals, each offering a unique topic for reflection every week, find a routine that suits you best to engage with *The Code of Contentment*. Whether it's on a quiet Sunday night or setting aside thirty minutes each week at a consistent time, establish that dedicated moment. We all lead busy lives, but even in the busiest and most stressful times, Jesus found solace in spending time with His Father (Luke 22:39-44). Learn from my past missteps; without intentional scheduling and planning, it's challenging to stay consistent in your walk with God. Be intentional with your time, candid with the questions posed, and authentic in your journal entries. Only then can you truly absorb and evolve within God's purpose for you.

Let's dive in. God is poised to communicate with you over the next year, but you need to be prepared to engage in honest dialogue with Him. It's that reciprocal relationship with the Father that He craves and that we all yearn for. Rest assured that the door is open today, and I hope *The Code of Contentment* empowers you to confidently step through it in the year ahead.

> **Quotable:** "If you don't plan to live the Christian life totally committed to knowing your God and to walking in obedience to Him, then don't begin; for this is what Christianity is all about. It is a change of citizenship, a change of governments, a change of allegiance. If you have no intention of letting Christ rule your life, then forget Christianity; it's not for you" (Kay Arthur).

> **What does scripture say?** "Commit your works to the Lord and your plans will be established" (Proverbs 16:3).

Reflection: Am I committed to spending the next year in the Word, in prayer, and in reflection every week? Reaffirm your commitment and thoughts here.

What is one goal I want to be intentional about accomplishing this week?

_____

_____

_____

_____

_____

What is one relationship I am going to focus on this week?

_____

_____

_____

_____

What is one thing I can do this week to better my physical and/or mental health?

_____

_____

_____

_____

_____

What am I grateful for in my life right now?

_____

_____

_____

_____

_____

Spend time in prayer following the PATH (praise, admit, thank, help).

LIFE IS SHORT.
GET UP EARLY.

Years ago, I consciously adopted the habit of waking up early—remarkably early. It struck me that the hours between 9:30 PM and 11:30 PM each evening were being squandered on mindless TV, aimless internet scrolling, unnecessary snacking, and other unproductive activities. Determined to reclaim these "garbage hours," I decided to shift them to the early morning. For many years, my wake-up time was a steadfast 4:21 AM, and more recently, it is settled on 4:50 AM. Despite the slight variations in the time, my commitment to rising early has remained unwavering for most of my adult life.

Let me pause here to say that I hate getting up early. People will sometimes remark to me, "Good for you, Paul, but I am not a morning person." Well, neither am I! The daily temptation to hit the snooze never goes away, but I know that the reward of those two precious hours each day far outweighs the extra sleep. It just takes commitment, discipline, and a desire to use those hours to better yourself.

Becoming an early riser, I assert, has been a transformative force in my life. Commencing my day before the sun, before the deluge of emails, and before the household stirs awake has given me a sacred span of uninterrupted and tranquil time that I never had when I was a night owl. Over the past fifteen years, I've harnessed these early hours for pursuits central to my well-being—primarily, faith and fitness. My daily regimen includes a workout (and, in more recent years, a cold plunge worked in) followed by a dedicated time of reflection, reading the Bible, and engaging in prayer. The specific nature of these practices has evolved, but the constancy of this routine has not faltered.

Just like a good meal is needed to give us energy for the day ahead, a regimented and intentional early morning routine can act like jet fuel for the rest of our day. While I don't contend that being an early riser is an indispensable key to success, I ardently believe that carving out those two precious hours each day for faith and fitness contributes indispensably to a well-rounded and balanced life. Give it a try. After all, what do you have to lose?

> **Quotable:** "The early morning has gold in its mouth" (Ben Franklin).
>
> **What does scripture say?** "O God, You are my God; Early will I seek You" (Psalm 63:1).
>
> **Reflection:** Am I front-loading my day with time in scripture and prayer? Am I having a hard time making time for God each day? If not, what habits must I adjust to make that happen this week?

Take time to reflect on your notes from last week. What worked and what didn't?

_____

_____

_____

_____

_____

What is one goal I want to be intentional about accomplishing this week?

_____

_____

_____

_____

_____

_____

What is one relationship I am going to focus on this week?

_____

_____

_____

_____

_____

What is one thing I can do this week to better my physical and/or mental health?

_____

_____

_____

_____

_____

What am I grateful for in my life right now?

_____

_____

_____

_____

Spend time in prayer following the PATH (praise, admit, thank, help).

EAT THE FROG

Embracing the timeless productivity principle that claims tackling the toughest task first thing in the morning, often referred to as "eating the frog," can significantly enhance your daily effectiveness. Reflecting on one of my early career experiences, I found myself immersed in a sales-driven role, specifically cold-calling, a task I genuinely disliked. I actually hated it. Despite the inevitability of confronting this challenging aspect of the job, I would often delay it and find other things to work on instead, unwittingly heightening my anxiety about the inevitable calls I was required to make.

This tendency to procrastinate on difficult tasks is a common phenomenon. Consider the reluctance to engage in a tough conversation with a colleague or the hesitation to address a habit in need of change. Unfortunately, postponing these challenges only exacerbates the root issues, fostering a breakdown of trust and complicating resolutions that could have been achieved by addressing concerns promptly. Said another way, procrastination kills progress.

Successful individuals, however, distinguish themselves by confronting difficult tasks head-on. They adeptly navigate the art of consistently "eating the frog," willingly embracing challenges throughout the day that others shy away from. This proactive approach yields results that many aspire to achieve. Instead of succumbing to the temptation of postponement, these high achievers equip themselves with a determination to dive in, transforming challenging situations into opportunities for growth and accomplishment. By adopting a mindset that prioritizes tackling demanding tasks promptly, you set the stage for continuous success, turning what may seem insurmountable into achievable milestones.

This philosophy, rooted in prioritization and proactive action, sets a powerful precedent for personal and professional growth. It's really a mindset shift that can propel you forward, empowering you to break the cycle of procrastination and take charge of your tasks and goals. The next time you are faced with a difficult challenge at work, a relationship that needs confronting, or a task you've been turning a blind eye to, don't delay. Jump in and flex that determination muscle. Soon, you'll find that eating the frog can become your most important meal of the day.

> **Quotable:** "Procrastination is opportunity's assassin" (Victor Kian).

> **What does scripture say?** "If anyone, then, knows the good they ought to do and doesn't do it, it is sin for them" (James 4:17).

> **Reflection:** What frog am I avoiding eating right now that I need to confront? What habits can I change or distractions can I remove to get better at eating my frogs?

Take time to reflect on your notes from last week. What worked and what didn't?

_____

_____

_____

_____

_____

What is one goal I want to be intentional about accomplishing this week?

_____

_____

_____

_____

_____

What is one relationship I am going to focus on this week?

_____

_____

_____

_____

_____

_____

What is one thing I can do this week to better my physical and/or mental health?

_____

_____

_____

_____

_____

What am I grateful for in my life right now?

_____

_____

_____

_____

Spend time in prayer following the PATH (praise, admit, thank, help).

WEEK 4

THE CASE FOR BRUTAL HONESTY

n June 2020, our world teetered on fragility. Our nation, grappling with the tumult of the COVID-19 pandemic for three months at that point, found itself ensnared in the chaos and uncertainty of the unknown. Amid this upheaval, the sparks of racial and social justice issues were kindled across the country following the tragic incident involving George Floyd in Minneapolis.

The resulting chaos swept through our nation, manifesting in riots and protests that spanned from coast to coast. Even my community, Sioux Falls, South Dakota, was not shielded as we navigated a tense night marred by rioting, assaults, arrests, and visible fractures in our once-cohesive community. It was one of the lowest points in my time as mayor.

On that tumultuous evening in Sioux Falls, as the riots unfolded, I took to the airwaves, and my emotions overcame me. From the emergency operations center, I had witnessed members of our community, some familiar faces among them, hurling rocks at police officers, making lewd gestures to passersby, and transforming what started as a peaceful protest into a night of lawlessness. In a moment of unfiltered candor, I addressed the community:

"Parents, if you have a kid between the ages of sixteen to twenty and don't know where they are right now, I have a pretty good idea where they might be. You need to get out here and drag them home."

While not the most eloquent speech, it came from a place of unvarnished truth, a bit of anger, and considerable frustration with the unfolding situation. The media ran that quote for days, and I later learned of several parents who heeded the advice, mobilized their efforts, and located their children to prevent them from escalating confrontations with our law enforcement community.

There are moments that call for sensitivity, calculation, and guardedness. However, there are also times when leaders must speak from the heart with brutal honesty, delivering hard truths that may be difficult for some to hear. Speaking with candor and emotion at times shows those you are leading that you care. Recognizing the right time for each approach can distinguish good leaders from great ones.

> **Quotable:** "Nothing in this world is harder than speaking the truth, nothing easier than flattery" (Fyodor Dostoevsky).

> **What does scripture say**? "He who speaks truth tells what is right, but a false witness, deceit" (Proverbs 12:17).

> **Reflection:** Do I avoid speaking the truth at times for fear of offending those who may disagree with me?

Take time to reflect on your notes from last week. What worked and what didn't?

_____

_____

_____

_____

_____

What is one goal I want to be intentional about accomplishing this week?

_____

_____

_____

_____

_____

What is one relationship I am going to focus on this week?

_____

_____

_____

_____

_____

_____

What is one thing I can do this week to better my physical and/or mental health?

_____

_____

_____

_____

_____

What am I grateful for in my life right now?

_____

_____

_____

_____

_____

Spend time in prayer following the P.A.T.H. (Praise, Admit, Thank, Help).

WEEK 5

THE COMPARISON TRAP

L iving in a society dominated by social media, it's nearly unavoidable to escape the curated highlight reels showcasing the seemingly flawless aspects of everyone's lives. Rarely do we witness the struggles—the marital spats, the breakdown of a car, the disheartening performance reviews, or a teenager grappling with addiction. Consequently, we inadvertently construct a distorted reality of those around us, convinced that their meticulously presented lives surpass our own on nearly every level.

This phenomenon propels us down the perilous path of constant comparison, fostering a destructive "if only" mentality. If only our spouse mirrored someone else's, if only our vacations matched theirs, if only our child excelled in sports like theirs—this loop of comparison becomes a relentless and damaging cycle.

Genuine contentment, however, emanates from an internal source, not external benchmarks set by others. There will always be individuals seemingly wealthier, with seemingly perfect families, careers free of hiccups, and bodies slightly more sculpted than ours. It's an incessant treadmill of comparison. The silver lining? We can step off this ride at any moment.

The key to peace and contentment lies not in perpetual comparison but in recognizing that our true identity is rooted in something beyond the transient offerings of this world. True solace is found in acknowledging our identity in Christ and his mark on our lives rather than fixating on worldly achievements.

Until we embrace this reality, the comparison trap will persist, ensnaring us in a cycle that hinders our personal growth and fulfillment. Society's steady drum beat telling us "you are not enough" is in direct conflict with the hope of the Gospel and the promise of salvation from a God who could care less about early achievements. Take time to reflect on that reality today, asking God to help you find contentment by breaking the chains of comparison.

> **Quotable:** "Every minute you spend wishing you had someone else's life, is a minute spent wasting yours" (Unknown).

> **What does scripture say?** "Keep your life free from love of money, and be content with what you have, for he has said, "I will never leave you nor forsake you" (Hebrews 13:5).

> **Reflection:** Who have I been comparing myself to recently? Why am I doing that? What steps can I take to find contentment in what God has blessed me with?

Take time to reflect on your notes from last week. What worked and what didn't?

_____

_____

_____

_____

_____

What is one goal I want to be intentional about accomplishing this week?

_____

_____

_____

_____

_____

What is one relationship I am going to focus on this week?

_____

_____

_____

_____

_____

_____

What is one thing I can do this week to better my physical and/or mental health?

_____

_____

_____

_____

_____

What am I grateful for in my life right now?

_____

_____

_____

_____

_____

Spend time in prayer following the P.A.T.H. (Praise, Admit, Thank, Help).

THE FALLACY OF SECULAR VS. CHRISTIAN WORK

've always regarded my work as a form of worship—a means of honoring God by applying my skills to the best of my abilities and serving those around me. In my perspective, every believer engages in full-time Christian ministry, irrespective of whether they've chosen career paths traditionally associated with pastors, missionaries, or "full-time Christian" roles. Whether you're a plumber, receptionist, or pharmacist, your work is considered full-time Christian service in the eyes of God. Remember, even Jesus spent about twenty years working as a carpenter—six times the duration of his three-year public ministry! While Scripture spends very little time on Jesus' pre-ministry life, I am confident of his kingdom's impact on those around him through his labor as a carpenter. There are times I long to learn more about those "working years" of his life!

For most of us, a significant portion of our waking hours will be dedicated to work. Failing to recognize the profound connection between our faith and our professional lives overlooks God's holistic plan for us. Our work and how we approach it should be seen as a means of honoring God through the unique gifts He has bestowed upon each of us. Never underestimate the significance of your role or think that you're not engaged in "real Christian work" simply because your career isn't traditionally labeled as Christian by the world. All work is an opportunity for worship, and each day is a chance to serve God and those around us by performing each task with excellence.

Understanding that our daily occupations are part of our spiritual journey allows us to align our efforts with our faith. It's about embracing the idea that our work can be a form of ministry—whether it's through acts of kindness, diligence, or integrity in the workplace. When we recognize this, our jobs become avenues to express our devotion and to contribute positively to the world around us. It's not just about the job title or the industry; it's about using our skills and talents to glorify God and bless others. Jesus' silent years in carpentry teach us that even in what seems like the mundane, there's an opportunity for profound impact and service to God.

> **Quotable:** "Faith gives you a concept of the dignity and worth of all work, even simple work, without which work could bore you" (Timothy Keller).

> **What does scripture say?** "The LORD God took the man and put him in the Garden of Eden to work it and take care of it" (Genesis 2:15).

> **Reflection:** How would my perspective at work change if I viewed it as worship to God? What is one thing I can do to be a stronger witness for Christ in my workplace?

Take time to reflect on your notes from last week. What worked and what didn't?

_____

_____

_____

_____

_____

What is one goal I want to be intentional about accomplishing this week?

_____

_____

_____

_____

_____

What is one relationship I am going to focus on this week?

_____

_____

_____

_____

_____

_____

What is one thing I can do this week to better my physical and/or mental health?

_____

_____

_____

_____

_____

What am I grateful for in my life right now?

_____

_____

_____

_____

_____

Spend time in prayer following the P.A.T.H. (Praise, Admit, Thank, Help).

KILLING DISTRACTIONS

I n an era saturated with distractions, the remarkable technological advancement of the mobile phone, though a marvel, paradoxically poses a significant challenge to our daily productivity. Astonishingly, the average American touches their phone a staggering 2,617 times daily, unlocking it approximately 150 times. These statistics undeniably demonstrate how smartphones can serve as formidable distractions in our daily lives.

A popular saying is that distractions are the enemies of greatness. When persistent diversions hinder our focus on a goal, achieving that goal becomes a formidable challenge, potentially rendering it unattainable. Beyond technological distractions, we grapple with relationship detours, unproductive habits (cue the Netflix binge), and even addictions that, left unaddressed, obstruct the realization of our fullest potential.

Personally, I've taken measures to mitigate a few of my own distractions, such as severing some challenging relationships, imposing limits on my own screen time, and relocating my home office to a less disruptive environment where I could focus more. Acknowledging that distractions are not inherently negative, the crucial realization lies in the ability to manage and control them. Without this mastery, unlocking our full potential will always remain a challenge.

However, managing distractions doesn't mean eradicating them entirely; it's about creating an environment that fosters focus. It involves strategic planning, setting boundaries, and developing the discipline to prioritize tasks. I've found that structuring my day, allocating specific time blocks for tasks, and implementing tech-free zones contribute significantly to minimizing distractions. Additionally, fostering a habit of mindfulness and practicing deep work techniques have been instrumental for me in combating distractions.

Moreover, recognizing that not all distractions are external is pivotal. Internal distractions, like self-doubt, overthinking, or fear of failure, can be equally detrimental to productivity. Cultivating self-awareness and practicing techniques like regular prayer or journaling help in managing these internal hurdles. With dedication, consistent practice, and intentional effort, we can transform distractions from roadblocks into stepping stones toward achieving our goals and aspirations.

> **Quotable:** "Keep your mind off the things you don't want by keeping it on the things you do want" (W. Clement Stone).

> **What does scripture say?** "Set your mind on things above, not on earthly things" (Colossians 3:2).

Reflection: Thinking about your own life, what is one distraction that you need to cut out in order to move forward with your goals?

Take time to reflect on your notes from last week. What worked and what didn't?

_____

_____

_____

_____

_____

What is one goal I want to be intentional about accomplishing this week?

_____

_____

_____

_____

_____

What is one relationship I am going to focus on this week?

_____

_____

_____

_____

What is one thing I can do this week to better my physical and/or mental health?

_____

_____

_____

_____

_____

What am I grateful for in my life right now?

_____

_____

_____

_____

Spend time in prayer following the P.A.T.H. (Praise, Admit, Thank, Help).

WEEK 8

TAKE THE FEEDBACK

vividly recall April of 2020, a period etched in my memory. Our community was grappling with the initial stages of the COVID-19 pandemic, and the tension was palpable. Sioux Falls, SD, found itself in the national spotlight as a major processing plant became one of the nation's first "COVID hot spots." Media from all over the country, recognizing our situation, inundated me with inquiries, emails, phone calls, and interview requests, all asking the question, "Mayor, what are you going to do?"

During this time, cities nationwide were implementing stay-at-home orders, urging residents to limit activities to essential ones and minimize contact with other people in order to curb the spread of the virus. Faced with the daunting task of navigating this unknown threat while feeling an immense responsibility for our community's safety, I contemplated a stay-at-home order for Sioux Falls and shared that idea publicly at a press conference. After all, if other cities were adopting such measures, shouldn't we follow suit.

Amidst this uncertainty, my friend Eric reached out to offer his support, recognizing the weight of my responsibilities. He prayed for me and, with genuine concern, questioned the wisdom of the proposed stay-at-home order. "Paul, so you think this is a good idea?" he asked, assuring me of his unwavering support for me but prompting me to consider the potential outcomes and efficacy of the plan.

Eric's call required courage, and it demanded courage for me to go against the prevailing public sentiment pushing for this stay-at-home action. Ultimately, I chose not to pursue the stay-at-home order, influenced in part by Eric's candid feedback. His words were timely, challenging to absorb, and unprompted, but precisely what I needed to hear at the time.

Leaders often seek feedback, yet when received, they may dismiss it, proceeding with their original intentions regardless. The lesson here is to embrace feedback, listen to those around you, and cultivate an inner circle of individuals who can provide honest insights and hold you accountable—even when it is hard to hear. Recognizing that we don't traverse this journey alone makes the burden significantly lighter.

> **Quotable:** "Average players want to be left alone. Good players want to be coached. Great players want to be told the truth" (Doc Rivers).

> **What does scripture say?** "As iron sharpens iron, so one person sharpens another" (Proverbs 27:17).

> **Reflection:** Who do I have in my life that can give me honest feedback? If no one, how can I develop a relationship with someone to keep me accountable and speak candid truth to me?

Take time to reflect on your notes from last week. What worked and what didn't?

_____

_____

_____

_____

_____

What is one goal I want to be intentional about accomplishing this week?

_____

_____

_____

_____

_____

What is one relationship I am going to focus on this week?

_____

_____

_____

_____

_____

_____

What is one thing I can do this week to better my physical and/or mental health?

_____

_____

_____

_____

_____

What am I grateful for in my life right now?

_____

_____

_____

_____

_____

Spend time in prayer following the P.A.T.H. (Praise, Admit, Thank, Help).

WEEK 9

FOSTERING UNITY IN DIVISIVE POLITICAL TIMES

Today, we find ourselves immersed in politically charged times, inundated daily with messages urging us to be outraged by the state of affairs. Social media, television broadcasts, radio personalities—all echo the sentiment that we should take sides on the current political landscape or respond fervently to the heightened racial and social tensions of recent years.

Amidst these loud opinions and the seemingly endless cacophony of keyboard warriors suggesting remedies for societal woes, I've had the profound privilege, as the mayor of Sioux Falls, SD, to guide a rapidly growing community. However, navigating the direction God is leading our city, state, and nation amid the political chaos is a perpetual challenge.

Rather than viewing these times as chaotic, I believe God is using them to demonstrate His control and power. In doing so, He offers Christians an unprecedented opportunity to be a beacon of light in what might appear as political darkness. It's easy to succumb to anger and engage in heated debates on social media regarding political candidates, election integrity, or policy positions.

What's challenging is extending empathy, understanding, and respect to those with differing views—a level of grace that can be exceptionally demanding. By demonstrating this grace and understanding, even in the face of adversity, we have a unique chance to stand out and exemplify what true listening and empathy can look like in a world starving for it.

I often reflect on the wisdom encapsulated in the quote, "Seek first to understand, then to be understood." When our default position in conversations is argumentative, our effectiveness in sharing our perspectives diminishes. Christ, throughout His earthly ministry, set the ultimate example for tolerance.

In John 8:7, Jesus implores, "Let him who is without sin among you be the first to throw a stone at her." In a world quick to react with anger and finger-pointing, we find this mandate increasingly challenging. While we are called to speak the truth, we must do so in love—the part we continually strive to uphold.

> **Quotable:** "My concern is not whether God is on our side; my greatest concern is to be on God's side, for God is always right" (Abraham Lincoln).

> **What does scripture say?** "My dear brothers and sisters, take note of this: Everyone should be quick to listen, slow to speak and slow to become angry" (James 1:19).

Reflection: How can I engage with others on political issues of the day in a manner that demonstrates understanding, love, and patience?

Take time to reflect on your notes from last week. What worked and what didn't?

_____

_____

_____

_____

_____

What is one goal I want to be intentional about accomplishing this week?

_____

_____

_____

_____

_____

What is one relationship I am going to focus on this week?

_____

_____

_____

_____

What is one thing I can do this week to better my physical and/or mental health?

_____

_____

_____

_____

_____

What am I grateful for in my life right now?

_____

_____

_____

_____

Spend time in prayer following the P.A.T.H. (Praise, Admit, Thank, Help).

CAREER PATIENCE

For a significant chunk of my career, I spearheaded a digital marketing agency, a small yet dynamic firm powered by an exceptional team, many of whom were young individuals leveraging their expertise in the emerging landscape of social media and digital technologies.

I clearly remember one performance review session with a talented team member who had been with us for just over a year or two. This individual showcased remarkable skills, excelling in her role, and clearly had a promising trajectory within our agency. However, during the review, it became evident she was frustrated by not being considered for upper-level management or partnership discussions.

At that point, as our company rapidly expanded and new leadership roles emerged, discussions mostly revolved around longer-tenured staff. Despite her relatively short tenure, she felt overlooked and undervalued. I conveyed her immense potential and assured her that opportunities for growth would naturally arise if she continued excelling in her current role and providing value to the company. Unfortunately, my advice didn't resonate, and within a few months, she decided to leave our company.

Careers unfold in unpredictable ways—long journeys marked by twists and turns. My own career journey is one I never could have imagined, but with the benefit of hindsight, I see God's plan through the chaos. One certainty I've gleaned is that exceptional individuals who consistently deliver quality work do get noticed, and opportunities inevitably present themselves. The timing might not always align with one's expectations, but they do come.

As the saying goes, "The days are long, but the years are short." Patience becomes crucial in navigating career progression. Keep doing the work diligently, put in the reps, stay hungry, and remain humble. Our work is worship to God, and doing it with both excellence and patience will create earthly success with even bigger opportunities for eternal significance. Ask God for patience today and trust that His plan is always perfect.

> **Quotable:** "When you get into a tight place and everything goes against you until it seems that you cannot hold on for a minute longer, never give up then, for that is just the place and time when the tide will turn" (Harriet Beecher Stowe).
>
> **What does scripture say?** "And let us not grow weary of doing good, for in due season we will reap, if we do not give up" (Galatians 6:9).
>
> **Reflection:** In what areas of my career do I need to have more patience and trust in God's plan?

Take time to reflect on your notes from last week. What worked and what didn't?

_____

_____

_____

_____

_____

What is one goal I want to be intentional about accomplishing this week?

_____

_____

_____

_____

_____

What is one relationship I am going to focus on this week?

_____

_____

_____

_____

_____

_____

What is one thing I can do this week to better my physical and/or mental health?

_____

_____

_____

_____

_____

What am I grateful for in my life right now?

_____

_____

_____

_____

_____

Spend time in prayer following the P.A.T.H. (Praise, Admit, Thank, Help).

KINDNESS IS
NOT WEAKNESS

P ause for a moment and think about the most exceptional manager you've ever worked with. What were the standout qualities that made this individual remarkable? It's likely that kindness was one of the key characteristics. Great managers possess an astute understanding of their team members' strengths and weaknesses. They empower their team while providing subtle guidance, all under an aura of kindness that fosters a sense of commitment from the employee in a desire not to let their manager down.

However, I've encountered managers who, while exceptionally kind, might have leaned too far in that direction. Surprising as it may seem, excessive kindness can pose challenges, especially when it lacks the ability to enforce discipline, navigate difficult conversations, and set clear and unwavering expectations. It's a fine balancing act that I still find myself working on daily.

I had the privilege of working for an outstanding manager named Mark. Mark's passion for both his work and his team was palpable, and he had an innate ability to make everyone feel valued and heard, regardless of their position within the organization.

During my interview with him, he imparted a crucial piece of advice: "Paul, your life priorities should be faith, family, and work—in that order."

Those words resonated deeply, signaling that I was about to go to work for someone who valued a robust work-life balance and genuinely cared about me as an individual, as well as for my spiritual growth. As I worked for him over the years, his demeanor rarely involved anger toward staff, vendors, or colleagues. When it did surface, it was a rare occurrence, signifying the gravity of the situation and the need for a course correction.

In today's workplace landscape, it's easy to misinterpret kindness as a sign of weakness. Some of the most resilient and effective leaders I've encountered have been among the kindest, but I also knew when it was time to be tough on issues. They adeptly blend various leadership qualities to bring out the best in their team and achieve the organization's overarching goals. A fine—but very achievable—balance.

> **Quotable:** "You can accomplish by kindness what you cannot by force" (Publilius Syrus).

> **What does scripture say?** "For everything there is a season, and a time for every matter under heaven: a time to be born, and a time to die; a time to plant, and a time to pluck up what is planted; a time to kill, and a time to heal; a time to break down, and a time to build up" (Ecclesiastes 3:1-3).

Reflection: Thinking about kindness, how do I honestly think my colleagues would describe me? How would I want them to describe me? What must I do to ensure the answers to these two questions are the same?

Take time to reflect on your notes from last week. What worked and what didn't?

_____

_____

_____

_____

_____

What is one goal I want to be intentional about accomplishing this week?

_____

_____

_____

_____

_____

What is one relationship I am going to focus on this week?

_____

_____

_____

_____

_____

What is one thing I can do this week to better my physical and/or mental health?

_____

_____

_____

_____

_____

What am I grateful for in my life right now?

_____

_____

_____

_____

_____

Spend time in prayer following the P.A.T.H. (Praise, Admit, Thank, Help).

PAUL TENHAKEN

BECOMING A WORLD CLASS PEOPLE NOTICER

Years ago, I engaged in a powerful Bible study with a small group of seven to eight men. Together, we worked through a curriculum that forced us into deep introspection, exploring our lives, earthly purpose, career callings, and more. This study stands out as one of the most spiritually enriching experiences I've ever had. Leading this group was a man named Randy—a gentle, soft-spoken middle-aged man. He exuded an uncommon depth of theological knowledge and authenticity that deeply resonated with me. From the first day I met him, I liked him and wanted to learn from him.

I once heard Randy described as a "world-class people noticer." He possessed an innate ability to discern those in need of attention. Amidst a crowded room, he effortlessly identified individuals who appeared uncomfortable or needed to be pulled into a conversation. Once he noticed someone in that state, he had this remarkable ability to focus entirely on them, instantly creating a sense of comfort and acknowledgment.

His memory lingers, and I often find myself reflecting on Randy and our time together. His untimely departure from this world left me wishing for more time with him, as I know our relationship would have gone deeper. He was the first to nudge me toward considering a career shift toward public service, a suggestion I initially resisted but eventually realized was right. He noticed something in me, and for that, I am forever grateful.

Our world is in dire need of more people like Randy—individuals who see beyond superficialities like bank accounts or social status. We need individuals who bypass the "what can they do for me" mindset in relationships, diving deeper to simply notice others at their core— as children bearing the image of God, craving encouragement and friendship. The coworker who remains withdrawn, the janitor we pass by every day, the elderly woman sitting alone at the coffee shop—these are the individuals worthy of our attention, yearning to be seen, waiting for someone to take notice of them. Look for these people this week.

> **Quotable:** "When we focus on ourselves, our world contracts as our problems and preoccupations loom large. But when we focus on others, our world expands. Our own problems drift to the periphery of the mind and so seem smaller, and we increase our capacity for connection—or compassionate action" (Daniel Goleman).

> **What does scripture say?** "But the Lord said to Samuel, 'Do not consider his appearance or his height, for I have rejected him. The Lord does not look at the things people look at. People look at

the outward appearance, but the Lord looks at the heart'" (1 Samuel 16:7).

Reflection: Who have you been noticing recently? How can you show kindness and love to them this week?

Take time to reflect on your notes from last week. What worked and what didn't?

_____

_____

_____

_____

_____

What is one goal I want to be intentional about accomplishing this week?

_____

_____

_____

_____

_____

What is one relationship I am going to focus on this week?

_____

_____

_____

_____

_____

What is one thing I can do this week to better my physical and/or mental health?

_____

_____

_____

_____

What am I grateful for in my life right now?

_____

_____

_____

_____

Spend time in prayer following the P.A.T.H. (Praise, Admit, Thank, Help).

WHAT IS THE PURPOSE OF WORK?

There have been countless mornings throughout my career where I've woken up with a lingering question: "What is the true purpose behind all this?" The routine of waking up, heading to work, returning home, sleeping, and repeating this cycle for years can, at times, seem rather mundane and, frankly, disheartening when work is perceived solely as a job and nothing more.

Yet, buried within this routine lies a deeper truth: the need to unearth a profound purpose within our work beyond the job tasks themselves. Genesis 2:15 reveals that "The Lord God took the man and put him in the Garden of Eden to work it and take care of it." He commanded Adam to work it, not just to consume it. At our core, as God's children, we're designed to work. Even God Himself engaged in work—creating the Garden of Eden, as illustrated in Genesis 2:2:

"By the seventh day God had finished the work he had been doing; so on the seventh day he rested from all his work."

Work's inclusion as one of the earliest mentions in the Bible is deliberate—it's meant to be seen as a form of service and worship to our Lord. When we begin to perceive our work as a means of honoring and glorifying God, it transforms into an avenue for expressing praise and joy to our almighty creator. Granted, let's not deny the existence of toilsome, tedious, and downright unenjoyable work experiences—we've all had our share of those. However, work encompasses seasons of sowing and reaping, moments of fulfillment and discouragement, and stretches of contentment and restlessness. Each of these seasons contributes to shaping us into the individuals God intended us to be, using work as the vehicle for that growth.

Regardless of these seasons, when we view our work as a form of worship and our workplaces as our mission fields, we have the opportunity to honor God in remarkable ways. I've discovered that adopting this perspective on work has been an immense source of encouragement for me, sustaining me through both the highs and lows of my career.

> **Quotable:** "Work becomes worship when you dedicate it to God and perform it with an awareness of his presence" (Rick Warren).

> **What does scripture say?** "Whatever you do, work at it with all your heart, as working for the Lord, not for human masters, since you know that you will receive an inheritance from the Lord as a reward. It is the Lord Christ you are serving" (Colossians 3:23-24).

> **Reflection:** How would my perspective on my job change if I viewed it as worship? If I currently don't have joy in my work, what must I do to regain it?

Take time to reflect on your notes from last week. What worked and what didn't?

_____

_____

_____

_____

_____

What is one goal I want to be intentional about accomplishing this week?

_____

_____

_____

_____

_____

What is one relationship I am going to focus on this week?

_____

_____

_____

_____

_____

_____

What is one thing I can do this week to better my physical and/or mental health?

_____

_____

_____

_____

_____

What am I grateful for in my life right now?

_____

_____

_____

_____

Spend time in prayer following the P.A.T.H. (Praise, Admit, Thank, Help).

QUARTER ONE CHECK-IN

Your year is now one-quarter over, and you have been following *The Code of Contentment* for three months. Congratulations! Take time now to look back over your journaling from the past three months. When you've finished doing that, review the following questions:

How am I doing with the goals I have set this past quarter? Where am I succeeding, and where am I failing?

_____

_____

_____

_____

_____

_____

What have been my biggest wins with the relationships I have focused on? What relationships do I need to improve?

_____

_____

_____

_____

_____

Being honest with myself, how do I feel about my physical and mental health right now? Have I made an impact on my overall wellness in the last quarter?

_____

_____

_____

_____

_____

Thinking about the last three months, what areas of my life am I most thankful for?

_____

_____

_____

_____

_____

WEEK 14

SHARPENING THE SPIRITUAL AX

F inding a spiritual rhythm in my life wasn't an immediate stride once I stepped into the workforce post-college. For years, I attempted to squeeze in moments for devotions and prayer whenever they could fit into my day—sometimes in the morning, during breaks at work, in my car over lunch, or before dozing off at night. However, my attempts at this scattered approach revealed that without a dedicated time and rhythm, my personal spiritual life would remain sporadic.

A study published in the 2019 American Journal of Medicine highlighted that individuals in good physical health follow highly routine health behaviors. Adopting a lifestyle change necessitates a consistent routine and the formation of habits—you can't anticipate improvements by exercising "when you can." Exercise requires a structured and scheduled approach to yield maximum effectiveness.

Likewise, spiritual well-being cannot be relegated to happenstance or treated as an "I'll get to it when I have time" activity. Nurturing spiritual growth demands discipline and routine to integrate it into your daily life.

It was when I established an early morning routine that everything shifted for me. Rising early, hitting a workout, dedicating time to read my Bible and pray, and then preparing for the day became my ritual. My day was simply off if I didn't begin with this routine. This practice of sharpening both my physical and spiritual axes in the morning infused me with a sense of energy and purpose that would be hard for me to find without this routine.

Crafting a structured spiritual rhythm is crucial in strengthening your relationship with God. When intentionally integrated into your routine rather than left to chance, this dedicated time with God offers an energy and fulfillment that ensures our axes remain sharp as we face each and every day as servants for the kingdom.

> **Quotable:** "The essence of meditation is a period of time set aside to contemplate the Lord, listen to Him, and allow Him to permeate our spirits" (Charles Stanley).

> **What does scripture say?** "This Book of the Law shall not depart from your mouth, but you shall meditate on it day and night, so that you may be careful to do according to all that is written in it. For then you will make your way prosperous, and then you will have good success" (Joshua 1:8).

> **Reflection:** How disciplined am I with spending time in scripture and in prayer? Are there roadblocks or distractions in my life I need to remove to become more faithful in this area?

Take time to reflect on your notes from last week. What worked and what didn't?

_____

_____

_____

_____

_____

What is one goal I want to be intentional about accomplishing this week?

_____

_____

_____

_____

_____

What is one relationship I am going to focus on this week?

_____

_____

_____

_____

_____

What is one thing I can do this week to better my physical and/or mental health?

_____

_____

_____

_____

_____

What am I grateful for in my life right now?

_____

_____

_____

_____

_____

Spend time in prayer following the P.A.T.H. (Praise, Admit, Thank, Help).

WEEK 15

YOUR EULOGIZED SELF

For the initial eighteen years of my career, I immersed myself in the marketing realm, particularly in digital marketing. In 2008, stumbling into entrepreneurship, I founded my own digital marketing agency just as the social media wave was starting to form. Back then, in the days of MySpace and Friendster, few companies comprehended how to leverage social media for their benefit. Being a digital native, I felt at ease navigating this space, and consequently, our company thrived and experienced rapid growth early on.

Yet, amidst this entrepreneurial journey and the company's success, the emptiness of mere earthly business triumphs became starkly evident. I often grappled with society's definition of business success—acquiring more clients, chasing wealth, expanding a brand, constantly reaching for the next pinnacle. I realized I was dedicating more time to cultivating my "LinkedIn Self" rather than focusing on my "Eulogized Self"—who I truly wanted to be and the impact I wished to leave behind.

This tension between my professional persona and the legacy I sought to create prompted me to make a significant shift. I decided to exit the business world and sell my company to embark on a journey into public office. The stirring within me, the call I felt from God to pursue public service, aligned perfectly with my desire to serve others and be a witness for the kingdom. Although the role of mayor differed vastly from that of an entrepreneur and, in many ways, proved more demanding, it presented an opportunity to center my focus on my deeper aspirations and the impact I aimed to make on those around me.

There's an old adage: "You never see a hearse pulling a U-Haul." In other words, all the material possessions and career achievements we accumulate will ultimately fade away. It's when we contemplate how we wish to be remembered and the impact we hope to have on the kingdom that we begin to see our career in a new and profound light.

> **Quotable:** "Living to create an earthly legacy is a short-sighted goal. A wiser use of time is to build an eternal legacy" (Unknown).

> **What does scripture say?** "But store up for yourselves treasures in heaven, where moths and vermin do not destroy, and where thieves do not break in and steal. For where your treasure is, there your heart will be also" (Matthew 6:20-21).

> **Reflection:** Spend a few minutes thinking about how you would like to be remembered when you pass. Does the way you're living match up with the words you hope will be spoken?

Take time to reflect on your notes from last week. What worked and what didn't?

_____

_____

_____

_____

_____

What is one goal I want to be intentional about accomplishing this week?

_____

_____

_____

_____

_____

What is one relationship I am going to focus on this week?

_____

_____

_____

_____

_____

_____

What is one thing I can do this week to better my physical and/or mental health?

_____

_____

_____

_____

_____

What am I grateful for in my life right now?

_____

_____

_____

_____

_____

Spend time in prayer following the P.A.T.H. (Praise, Admit, Thank, Help).

WHAT ARE YOU PASSIONATE ABOUT?

Throughout my career, I've conducted numerous interviews for a variety of positions I was hiring for at the time. Initially, I thought I had the interview process down to a science, with a set of standard questions: "What are your strengths? Your weaknesses? A moment you're proud of? What do you like about your current job? Tell me about someone you admire." However, I soon realized that while these questions were crucial, they didn't delve into the essence of who the candidate truly was.

While I gained insights into their technical skills, qualifications, and potential fit for the role, I was missing a vital piece—their personality and character. Discovering "who" the person is often outweighs understanding "what" they'll do within the company. Today, there's one question I ask that consistently reveals the core of each candidate and unravels what drives them.

"Tell me what you are passionate about?"

When this question arises, it's fascinating to witness the transformation in candidates. Their faces light up, and a genuine smile emerges as they speak about something that sets their soul on fire—whether it's rescuing animals, contributing to their church choir, engaging in youth soccer, mentoring inmates, perfecting their golf game, or leading a Bible study.

This question not only unveils their passions but also allows me to gauge how they express that passion. Does their life revolve solely around work, or do they cultivate a well-rounded existence centered on their passions? Are they individuals with depth, or are they unknowingly heading toward career burnout due to a lack of a personal/professional balance?

A person's passions can reveal a great deal about them and offer glimpses into their future trajectory. You just need to ask.

> **Quotable:** "Light yourself on fire with passion and people will come from miles to watch you burn" (John Welsley).

> **What does scripture say?** "Never be lacking in zeal, but keep your spiritual fervor, serving the Lord" (Romans 12:11).

> **Reflection:** What are you truly passionate about? Are you able to use your passions for an eternal purpose and witness for Christ?

Take time to reflect on your notes from last week. What worked and what didn't?

_____

_____

_____

_____

_____

What is one goal I want to be intentional about accomplishing this week?

_____

_____

_____

_____

_____

What is one relationship I am going to focus on this week?

_____

_____

_____

_____

_____

_____

What is one thing I can do this week to better my physical and/or mental health?

_____

_____

_____

_____

_____

What am I grateful for in my life right now?

_____

_____

_____

_____

_____

Spend time in prayer following the P.A.T.H. (Praise, Admit, Thank, Help).

ACCEPTING BEING UNCOMFORTABLE

Running for public office ranks among the most challenging professional endeavors I've ever pursued. It requires a level of vulnerability that exposes you to public scrutiny, where your beliefs, appearance, speech, and even your previous career choices are subjected to judgment. Politics isn't for the faint of heart, and it's no surprise that this scrutiny often discourages people from stepping into the arena.

The fear of facing such intense scrutiny was a prevailing force throughout many years of my career. Uncomfortable situations prompted me to seek alternative paths. If a job became difficult, I sought a new one. Confrontation with a friend? I'd slowly drift away from that friendship. Public speaking anxiety? I'd find any reason to avoid speaking engagements. In essence, I would choose comfort over discomfort every chance I got.

However, it wasn't until I ventured into the realm of public service that I realized the transformative power of embracing discomfort. Growth doesn't sprout from complacency; it flourishes when we confront challenging environments, allowing us to discover more about ourselves. Some will go so far as to say the only time we really grow as individuals is when we step into a season of uncomfortability. Through the discomfort of public service, my faith has deepened, empathy for my community has grown, and I've developed a resilience that comfort could never have fostered. In an odd way, I now tend to seek out uncomfortable circumstances, knowing how they stretch my personal canvas.

Comfort in discomfort yields remarkable personal growth. Embrace the challenges God places in your life and the invaluable lessons they bring. They are there for a reason, and in embracing them, you will have a front-row seat to watching your own evolution unfold.

> **Quotable:** "The truth is that our finest moments are most likely to occur when we are feeling deeply uncomfortable, unhappy, or unfulfilled. For it is only in such moments, propelled by our discomfort, that we are likely to step out of our ruts and start searching for different ways or truer answers" (M. Scott Peck).

> **What does scripture say?** "Let's not get tired of doing good, because in time we'll have a harvest if we don't give up" (Galatians 6:9).

> **Reflection:** In what areas of your life are you afraid to get uncomfortable? How may that be limiting God's purpose for you?

Take time to reflect on your notes from last week. What worked and what didn't?

_____

_____

_____

_____

_____

What is one goal I want to be intentional about accomplishing this week?

_____

_____

_____

_____

_____

What is one relationship I am going to focus on this week?

_____

_____

_____

_____

_____

What is one thing I can do this week to better my physical and/or mental health?

_____

_____

_____

_____

_____

What am I grateful for in my life right now?

_____

_____

_____

_____

_____

Spend time in prayer following the P.A.T.H. (Praise, Admit, Thank, Help).

THE POWER OF
RECOGNITION

As humans, I believe we all possess an inherent inclination to want to lend a hand and support others. Call me an eternal optimist, but I believe people are wired to want to help other people. While not everyone acts on this innate trait daily, I believe it's woven into our nature by our creator. Moreover, most individuals relish acknowledgment for their good deeds. Whether it's holding the door open for someone, meeting a crucial deadline at work, fulfilling a child's wish, or volunteering in the community, receiving recognition and a word of thanks when you perform a task for someone is always uplifting.

A recent Harvard Business Review study revealed that top indicators of employee motivation—satisfaction, engagement, commitment, and the intention to stay—were more influenced by positive recognition than by salary. People hunger for recognition! This study suggests that acknowledging and appreciating those around you regularly, in combination with the power of a kind word, may hold greater value than monetary rewards.

In my own routine, I dedicate time each week to reflect on recent meetings or community engagements. I then write at least three handwritten notes, expressing gratitude and recognition for those interactions or sending notes to those who I believe could benefit from a kind word. It could be for a diligent server at a lunch meeting, an aspiring local entrepreneur, or a dedicated teacher whose efforts deserve acknowledgment. While texts or emails are convenient, I've found that nothing surpasses the impact of a handwritten note.

Kindness and recognition are potent superpowers within each of us, yet they often remain untapped. If you're seeking a competitive edge in both business and life, start recognizing people around you simply to uplift them. For me, it's one of the easiest ways to show the kindness of Christ to those who have been brought into my life.

> **Quotable:** "There is no greater joy than showing thanks and appreciation to someone who can do nothing for you in return" (Unknown).

> **What does scripture say?** "We always thank God for all of you and continually mention you in our prayers" (1 Thessalonians 1:2).

> **Reflection:** How can you use the power of recognition to show the love of Christ to someone around you this week? Who will you specifically seek to lift up?

Take time to reflect on your notes from last week. What worked and what didn't?

_____

_____

_____

_____

_____

What is one goal I want to be intentional about accomplishing this week?

_____

_____

_____

_____

_____

What is one relationship I am going to focus on this week?

_____

_____

_____

_____

_____

_____

What is one thing I can do this week to better my physical and/or mental health?

_____

_____

_____

_____

_____

What am I grateful for in my life right now?

_____

_____

_____

_____

_____

Spend time in prayer following the P.A.T.H. (Praise, Admit, Thank, Help).

LOVING YOUR HATERS

The term "haters" emerged in the mid-1990s during the rise of hip-hop, becoming a mainstream descriptor for those who aggressively criticize and disparage others. My friend and author Jon Gordon coined "haters" as an acronym: Having Anger Toward Everyone Reaching Success. Today, it's a widely used motivational term, particularly for those aiming to overcome the skepticism and negativity of others in their lives.

Throughout my years in public service, encountering critics has been inevitable. Elected officials often receive plenty of praise and blame, even for matters they have limited control over. While accepting praise poses a different kind of challenge, dealing with blame presents a very different story.

Jesus faced his own share of critics during his time on earth. The Pharisees consistently sought to entrap him in his words and distort his actions, attempting to undermine his ministry. Yet, Jesus responded with calm, truthfulness, and remarkable wisdom. Even in the face of hostility, he responded with candid yet poised remarks, exposing their hypocrisy (as detailed in Matthew 26, for example). Instead of engaging in a back-and-forth, he exemplified the approach we should follow when confronted by modern-day critics seeking to undermine our faith and actions.

Encountering detractors is an inevitable part of life for nearly all of us, with people attempting to discredit who we are and what we stand for. Fortunately, Scripture provides us with a perfect blueprint through Jesus' example on how to respond to such challenges.

In today's world, where social media and online platforms amplify criticisms, handling detractors requires both resilience and grace. Jesus' response to critics showcased not only his unwavering faith but also a composed, insightful approach that didn't escalate conflicts but rather brought clarity and truth. Following this example means responding to hostility with compassion, addressing false accusations with integrity, and remaining steadfast in our convictions without getting embroiled in unnecessary conflicts. It's about channeling our energies into what's truly valuable—faith, truth, and living out our purpose—rather than being derailed by the negativity of others.

> **Quotable:** "An entire sea of water can't sink a ship unless it gets inside the ship. Similarly, the negativity of the world can't put you down unless you allow it to get inside you" (Goi Nasu).

> **What does scripture say?** "Bless those who persecute you; bless and do not curse them" (Romans 12:14).

> **Reflection:** Are there people in your life who continually seek to tear you down? How can you deal with them in a Christ-like manner?

Take time to reflect on your notes from last week. What worked and what didn't?

_____

_____

_____

_____

_____

What is one goal I want to be intentional about accomplishing this week?

_____

_____

_____

_____

_____

What is one relationship I am going to focus on this week?

_____

_____

_____

_____

_____

What is one thing I can do this week to better my physical and/or mental health?

_____

_____

_____

_____

_____

What am I grateful for in my life right now?

_____

_____

_____

_____

_____

Spend time in prayer following the P.A.T.H. (Praise, Admit, Thank, Help).

WEEK 20

HEALTH IS WEALTH

When we mention "wealth" in society, the immediate association is with money. While technically accurate, what if we considered wealth in a more expansive sense, encompassing not only financial riches but also encompassing one's physical, emotional, and mental well-being?

I've observed numerous individuals, both personally close and more distant acquaintances, living lives centered on accumulating material wealth and possessions, often achieved at the cost of their physical health. Society frequently glorifies the "hustle" mentality—long work hours, a win-at-all-costs mindset in business—that often results in overlooked consequences like fractured relationships, idolizing work, and health issues stemming from stress, poor diet, lack of exercise, and other factors.

As cliché as it sounds, we possess just one body that demands our care. While wealth might allow us to upgrade vehicles or homes, no amount of financial gain can swap out a neglected, deteriorating body. Hospitals are filled with people living with regret, wishing they had stopped smoking, had eaten healthier, or had managed stress more effectively. Nurturing our bodies as Scripture calls for, treating them as sacred temples, ensures that we honor God with each day granted to us.

Author Denis Waitley aptly points out, "Time and health are two precious assets that we don't recognize and appreciate until they have been depleted." Those words are incredibly powerful. Let's pay homage to God by tending to our bodies with care and acknowledging them as the physical and spiritual temples they are meant to be.

> **Quotable:** "Good health is not something we can buy. However, it can be an extremely valuable savings account" (Anne Wilson Schaef).

> **What does scripture say?** "Do you not know that your bodies are temples of the Holy Spirit, who is in you, whom you have received from God? You are not your own; you were bought at a price. Therefore honor God with your bodies" (I Corinthians 6:19-20).

> **Reflection:** Do you think of your body as a temple of the Holy Spirit? What changes do you need to make in your life to better honor God in taking care of your temple?

Take time to reflect on your notes from last week. What worked and what didn't?

_____

_____

_____

_____

_____

What is one goal I want to be intentional about accomplishing this week?

_____

_____

_____

_____

_____

What is one relationship I am going to focus on this week?

_____

_____

_____

_____

What is one thing I can do this week to better my physical and/or mental health?

_____

_____

_____

_____

_____

What am I grateful for in my life right now?

_____

_____

_____

_____

_____

Spend time in prayer following the P.A.T.H. (Praise, Admit, Thank, Help).

WEEK 21

DEVELOPING A SABBATH RHYTHM

D uring my childhood, our household embraced the concept of honoring the Sabbath (Sunday) in a manner true to Biblical teachings. Sundays were dedicated to church attendance, marked by morning and evening services. The afternoons were reserved for quiet moments, naps, visits to grandma's house, and family-focused activities. It was a day absent of store visits, work commitments, or sports and other extracurricular pursuits—a genuine day of worship and relaxation.

In Genesis 2, we learn of God's act of resting on the seventh day, sanctifying and blessing it as a special day—a reminder for us to rest and reflect on our Maker. Recognizing that even God took a break from His work, this act of rest served as a blueprint for our own need for rest and rejuvenation.

Over time, I've become an advocate for what some term a "Sabbath rhythm." It's a less rigid interpretation of Sabbath, shifting from strict observance on Sundays to a more practical approach. This involves developing spiritual practices and rhythms to find rest throughout the week without sacrificing some of the special elements—such as church worship—that only Sunday can bring. While there's no definitive formula for Sabbath rest, I've discovered that integrating periods of rest and worship daily, weekly, and annually offers ongoing spiritual renewal. It's a departure from waiting until exhaustion sets in, refilling the tank, running full tilt, and then repeating the cycle.

Sunday remains a special day in my home—a day for worship, reflection, and, yes, those Sunday naps are still a tradition. However, by cultivating a Sabbath rhythm that extends beyond Sundays alone, incorporating it into the entire week, we can ensure that the rest and reflection God intends for us are always accessible and deeply ingrained into our daily lives.

> **Quotable:** "When you abide with God in Sabbath, an unshakable confidence shines from the inside out, enticing others toward the gift of rest as well" (Shelly Miller).

> **What does scripture say?** "For thus said the Lord God, the Holy One of Israel, 'In returning and rest you shall be saved; in quietness and in trust shall be your strength'" (Isaiah 30:15).

> **Reflection:** Has Sunday become "just another day" for you? What changes can you make to not only honor Sunday, but also build a Sabbath rhythm all week long?

Take time to reflect on your notes from last week. What worked and what didn't?

_____

_____

_____

_____

_____

What is one goal I want to be intentional about accomplishing this week?

_____

_____

_____

_____

_____

What is one relationship I am going to focus on this week?

_____

_____

_____

_____

_____

_____

What is one thing I can do this week to better my physical and/or mental health?

_____

_____

_____

_____

_____

What am I grateful for in my life right now?

_____

_____

_____

_____

_____

Spend time in prayer following the P.A.T.H. (Praise, Admit, Thank, Help)

WEEK 22

W.W.J.D.

Back in the 1990s, there was a widespread trend where nearly everyone seemed to be wearing those iconic "W.W.J.D" bracelets. The acronym stood for "What Would Jesus Do?"—a mantra that resonated strongly among both teens and adults during that decade. Those bracelets, a symbol of that movement, might still be tucked away somewhere in my home if I searched hard enough.

The roots of the W.W.J.D. movement trace back to the early 1900s, following the widespread popularity of Charles Sheldon's book, "In His Steps: What Would Jesus Do?" It's evident that for decades, the question of how Jesus would handle daily situations has been a guiding principle for believers in their day-to-day actions.

In our professional lives, we often face moral and ethical dilemmas that can tempt us. Should I tweak the numbers in this proposal for a better commission? Do I exaggerate a colleague's flaws to gain a promotional edge? Would the company notice if I kept these airline miles for myself despite it going against policy? What if I listed an MBA on my resume, even though I was a few credits short—would anyone really care?

There are actions that violate the law, and then there are those that, while not illegal, certainly cross ethical boundaries. It's in these latter scenarios that we need a litmus test to distinguish right from wrong. For me, the W.W.J.D. test has been a guiding principle, steering me through a maze of leadership challenges and ensuring that my words and actions in the workplace honor God. While it's not foolproof, I wholeheartedly recommend the W.W.J.D. test to anyone seeking moral clarity and guidance when faced with difficult decisions at work.

> **Quotable:** "If Jesus sets the divine standard for morality, I could now have an unwavering foundation for my choices and decisions, rather than basing them on the ever-shifting sands of expediency and self-centeredness" (Lee Strobel).

> **What does scripture say?** "For to this you have been called, because Christ also suffered for you, leaving you an example, so that you might follow in his steps" (1 Peter 2:21).

> **Reflection:** What decision-making criteria do you use when faced with a moral or ethical dilemma? How can you apply the W.W.J.D. test this week in your life?

Take time to reflect on your notes from last week. What worked and what didn't?

_____

_____

_____

_____

_____

What is one goal I want to be intentional about accomplishing this week?

_____

_____

_____

_____

_____

What is one relationship I am going to focus on this week?

_____

_____

_____

_____

What is one thing I can do this week to better my physical and/or mental health?

_____

_____

_____

_____

_____

What am I grateful for in my life right now?

_____

_____

_____

_____

_____

Spend time in prayer following the P.A.T.H. (Praise, Admit, Thank, Help).

SUNDAY NIGHT BLUES

E arly in my career, I vividly recall times when I would battle the weekly case of Sunday night blues. Sometimes, it even started on Saturday, that sinking feeling that the weekend was slipping away and Monday was fast approaching. Dissatisfaction with my career often led to an impending sense of dread about the workweek ahead. Some Sundays, I was admittedly a pretty miserable person to be around.

The Sunday night blues are often a symptom of more than just a job we don't enjoy. When we hinge our happiness solely on our job or employer, those blues become almost inevitable. The good news is there are simple steps we can take to change our perspective on the workweek, making Monday a day we look forward to instead of one we dread.

- Start seeing work as a "get to" rather than a "have to." Recognize that having an employment opportunity, which millions around the world might never have, is an incredible privilege and can drastically shift your outlook.
- Even if your current job isn't fulfilling, understand that it's a step, not the final destination. God often uses our present employment as a stepping stone for our future endeavors.
- Consider your work as an act of worship. How can you honor and glorify God by giving your best, even in a job that might not bring you joy? Whether you're a meat packer, electrician, salesperson, or barista, performing your duties with excellence is a form of worship, a noble responsibility, and an honor.

Colossians 3:23 reminds us, "Whatever you do, work heartily, as for the Lord and not for men, knowing that from the Lord you will receive the inheritance as your reward. You are serving the Lord Christ." Though we may not always relish our Monday morning tasks, finding solace in knowing that God sees us and has called us to this work encourages us to do it with excellence, ultimately serving Him as we tackle our Mondays and carrying that service to Him throughout the entire week.

Quotable: ""Every day is different, and some days are better than others, but no matter how challenging the day, I get up and live it" (Muhammad Ali).

What does scripture say? "For I know the plans I have for you," declares the LORD, "plans to prosper you and not to harm you, plans to give you hope and a future" (Jeremiah 29:11).

Reflection: If starting a new work week is a challenge for you, what can you do to reframe your perspective on work as worship to God?

Take time to reflect on your notes from last week. What worked and what didn't?

_____

_____

_____

_____

_____

What is one goal I want to be intentional about accomplishing this week?

_____

_____

_____

_____

_____

What is one relationship I am going to focus on this week?

_____

_____

_____

_____

_____

What is one thing I can do this week to better my physical and/or mental health?

_____

_____

_____

_____

_____

What am I grateful for in my life right now?

_____

_____

_____

_____

_____

Spend time in prayer following the P.A.T.H. (Praise, Admit, Thank, Help).

GOD AS CEO

vividly remember a crucial turning point in my entrepreneurial journey when I shifted from seeing myself as the CEO to recognizing God as the true CEO. At about the six or seven-year mark of my company, I began to realize how often I referred to it as "my" business, "my" clients, and "my" success. Looking back, I cringe at how self-centered I must have sounded. It was a friend who pointed out that my company wasn't really mine; rather, it was God's, and I was entrusted to manage it for a while. What a perspective shift that was for me.

That revelation transformed how I viewed business. I initiated a speaker series called "God as CEO" to challenge fellow business leaders and entrepreneurs to adopt this mindset. I aimed to encourage faith-based mission statements, some level of corporate tithing, and finding ways to integrate faith into the workplace respectfully and non-intrusively. My litmus test became: "If God walked into my company today and observed, would He be proud to call it His own?"

Balancing a faith-based focus in a company without excluding employees of different beliefs is a delicate task. When potential employees asked about our faith-based culture, I made it clear that they didn't need to share our beliefs to work here, but they should be comfortable with the idea that the company operates under God's guidance. Would an employment lawyer endorse this approach? Perhaps not, but I felt aligned with this approach in honoring God.

When we acknowledge God as the CEO of our business, we approach work with a perspective more focused on honoring God and serving others than just chasing profits and earthly success metrics. It's about making a kingdom impact through our work, serving those we've been entrusted to serve.

> **Quotable:** "Most Christians are more than content to live out their lives surrounded by the trappings of our world, rather than to risk losing them in becoming a radical Christian. A radical Christian (by my definition) is one who will put God first in all decisions, even when putting God first is costly. In the business world, this means putting God first even when doing so costs money. That is true freedom—spiritual freedom—as opposed to business bondage" (Larry Burkett).

> **What does scripture say?** "For I am not ashamed of the gospel, because it is the power of God that brings salvation to everyone who believes" (Romans 1:16).

> **Reflection:** How would your perspective on work change if you viewed God as the top executive in your company?

Take time to reflect on your notes from last week. What worked and what didn't?

_____

_____

_____

_____

_____

What is one goal I want to be intentional about accomplishing this week?

_____

_____

_____

_____

_____

What is one relationship I am going to focus on this week?

_____

_____

_____

_____

_____

_____

What is one thing I can do this week to better my physical and/or mental health?

_____

_____

_____

_____

_____

What am I grateful for in my life right now?

_____

_____

_____

_____

_____

Spend time in prayer following the P.A.T.H. (Praise, Admit, Thank, Help).

SETBACKS BEFORE COMEBACKS

Careers can be a rollercoaster ride, full of exhilarating highs and daunting lows, where our envisioned path can sometimes clash head-on with a different reality. Fresh out of college, armed with a web design degree and an unwavering work ethic, I landed an interview at a prestigious ad agency, confident I could make a meaningful impact at the company. I had the skills to do the job, the degree to back it up, and the desire to make my future employer incredibly successful. It was painfully evident, though, that this interview was a formality. Despite my best efforts to showcase my skills and hunger to contribute, I was swiftly dismissed and advised I may be better off seeking a basic typesetting job somewhere to "get my feet wet." I was angry, crushed, and determined all at the same time.

In the following years, I started to find my career stride. Even with some early success and growth of my company, I still couldn't erase the memory of that initial rejection nearly a decade earlier and the feeling like I had something to prove. It lingered, a constant reminder of a setback that stung deeply at the time. Looking back, it's intriguing how enduring that rejection was, and still is, in my memory.

They say setbacks pave the way for comebacks. Life often tosses curveballs and workplace disappointments that can make us question our choices and career paths. But I've learned that God doesn't err. He has a meticulously crafted plan for each of us, even when the road seems winding and hard to decipher. Instead of viewing challenges as roadblocks, seeing them as opportunities for growth can shift our perspective and ignite the drive to propel forward. Every hurdle is a chance to refine ourselves for what lies ahead. As the saying goes, you win some, and you *learn* some. Keeping that perspective is key to maintaining a forward-focused career path.

> **Quotable:** "Your ability to face setbacks and disappointments without giving up will be the measure of your ability to succeed" (Calvin Coolidge).

> **What does scripture say?** "Count it all joy, my brothers, when you meet trials of various kinds, for you know that the testing of your faith produces steadfastness. And let steadfastness have its full effect, that you may be perfect and complete, lacking in nothing" (James 1:2-4).

> **Reflection:** What is a recent setback you have experienced in your personal or professional life? How would you rate the way you responded to it?

Take time to reflect on your notes from last week. What worked and what didn't?

_____

_____

_____

_____

_____

What is one goal I want to be intentional about accomplishing this week?

_____

_____

_____

_____

_____

What is one relationship I am going to focus on this week?

_____

_____

_____

_____

_____

_____

What is one thing I can do this week to better my physical and/or mental health?

_____

_____

_____

_____

_____

What am I grateful for in my life right now?

_____

_____

_____

_____

_____

Spend time in prayer following the P.A.T.H. (Praise, Admit, Thank, Help).

NO 😊

THE JOY OF NO

Wanting to be liked and needed is a pretty universal human desire. Early in my career, if someone asked me to jump, I'd already be mid-air before they finished the question. Saying yes to every opportunity that came my way was my go-to move. I'd teach Sunday School, serve on boards, help non-profits—you name it, if I was asked, I was in.

But then reality hit. My schedule became a Jenga tower of commitments, and I was stretched thin like butter over too much bread. Saying yes to everything meant my personal life took a nosedive. Board meetings chomped away at quality time with my wife, and non-essential work commitments clashed with potential networking opportunities that were of much higher value. When I said yes to something, it meant I was saying no to something or someone else.

Then, enlightenment struck. I started to treat my time like it was a bag of gold. I mean, time is money, right? Putting a price tag on each hour of my day helped me see the value of what I was giving away with each yes. Suddenly, I was more selective, guarding my hours like a watchdog and only saying yes to commitments that were worthy of the value of my time.

Sure, you can always chase more cash, but time? Once it's gone, it's gone. Even Bill Gates and Beyoncé get the same twenty-four hours a day as we all do. When I became a choosy time-spender, committing only to things I was genuinely passionate about and where I knew I could make a real difference, I unlocked a newfound freedom.

Now? Life's more balanced, relationships are stronger, and my impact feels more intentional. Don't just say yes for the sake of it or because you are honored to have been asked—your time's too precious for that, and my friend, God has too many other things He is preparing for you!

> **Quotable:** "People think focus means saying yes to the thing you've got to focus on. But that's not what it means at all. It means saying no to the hundred other good ideas that there are. You have to pick carefully. I'm actually as proud of the things we haven't done as the things I have done. Innovation is saying no to 1,000 things" (Steve Jobs).

> **What does scripture say?** "Yet the news about him spread all the more, so the crowds of people came to hear him and to be healed of their sicknesses. But Jesus often withdrew to a lonely place and prayed" (Luke 5:15-16).

> **Reflection:** Where do you need to start saying no in your life so you can begin saying yes to what God has in store for you?

Take time to reflect on your notes from last week. What worked and what didn't?

_____

_____

_____

_____

_____

What is one goal I want to be intentional about accomplishing this week?

_____

_____

_____

_____

_____

What is one relationship I am going to focus on this week?

_____

_____

_____

_____

_____

_____

What is one thing I can do this week to better my physical and/or mental health?

_____

_____

_____

_____

_____

What am I grateful for in my life right now?

_____

_____

_____

_____

_____

Spend time in prayer following the P.A.T.H. (Praise, Admit, Thank, Help).

QUARTER TWO CHECK-IN

Your year is now half over, and you have been following *The Code of Contentment* for six months. Congratulations! Take time now to look back over your journaling from the past three months. When you've finished doing that, review the following questions:

How am I doing with the goals I have set this past quarter? Where am I succeeding, and where am I failing?

_____

_____

_____

_____

_____

_____

What have been my biggest wins with the relationships I have focused on? What relationships do I need to improve?

_____

_____

_____

_____

Being honest with myself, how do I feel about my physical and mental health right now? Have I made an impact on my overall wellness in the last quarter?

_____

_____

_____

_____

Thinking about the last three months, what areas of my life am I most thankful for?

_____

_____

_____

_____

_____

WEEK 27

LEARNING TO FORGIVE

Navigating the COVID-19 pandemic during 2020 was like attempting to wrestle an avalanche into submission—it felt impossible. The uncertainty, the fear, the sheer anger echoing across our communities, nation, and world was all-consuming. Even as I write these words, it still gives me a feeling of anxiety reflecting on the tension of that year.

I was thrust into the spotlight as a mayor, expected to shield our city from the invisible threat of a pandemic. Looking back, the strategies we banked on to help keep our community safe were promising based on the information and understanding we had at the time, but ultimately fragile and largely ineffective. Trying to keep everyone safe while still allowing for personal decisions to be made became an Atlas-sized weight on my shoulders.

Opinions sprouted like weeds, and everyone became a self-appointed expert, generously sharing their thoughts. Some well-intentioned advice felt more like a stab in the back. Friends, church members, community allies—everyone had a prescription for how I should handle things and often shared it in a less-than-professional way. I was so sick of the often angry advice that many were giving me that, eventually, I found myself developing my own anger over the situation.

It took time, but I learned to see beyond the harsh words, to peer into the hearts of those flinging them. I began to ask, "What's behind this? What's driving this angst?" rather than jumping to, "Why are you being so rude?" It was a shift from anger to empathy, understanding that their words were often born from deeper wells of fear or concern on the issues being presented by the issue of the day.

This journey through the pandemic and the aftermath gave me a heart that was more forgiving and understanding than before. It's not easy, but forgiveness became my secret weapon, unshackling me from the weight of grudges, the angry words, and the hurtful actions. Forgiveness can be a potent tool if wielded right—a key to unlocking a more optimistic and freer future from the shackles of holding a grudge.

> **Quotable:** ""Forgiveness is not a feeling; it is a commitment. It is a choice to show mercy, not to hold the offense up against the offender. Forgiveness is an expression of love" (Gary Chapman).

> **What does scripture say**? "Get rid of all bitterness, rage and anger, brawling and slander, along with every form of malice. Be kind and compassionate to one another, forgiving each other, just as in Christ God forgave you" (Ephesians 4:31-32).

PAUL TENHAKEN

Reflection: Do you hold grudges and have a hard time forgiving? Spend time today thinking about someone you need to forgive and consider acting on it.

Take time to reflect on your notes from last week. What worked and what didn't?

_____

_____

_____

_____

_____

What is one goal I want to be intentional about accomplishing this week?

_____

_____

_____

_____

_____

What is one relationship I am going to focus on this week?

_____

_____

_____

_____

_____

What is one thing I can do this week to better my physical and/or mental health?

_____

_____

_____

_____

_____

What am I grateful for in my life right now?

_____

_____

_____

_____

_____

Spend time in prayer following the P.A.T.H. (Praise, Admit, Thank, Help).

BECOMING A CHEERFUL RECEIVER

Before my tenure as the thirty-second mayor of Sioux Falls, I had a great journey as an entrepreneur—an adventure that had many challenges and triumphs. Among the countless perks, the income allowed my family a life of comfort and stability. Grateful doesn't quite capture the depth of appreciation I had for the opportunities my career provided. (Funny enough, it was this very feeling of comfort that eventually nudged me to leave my company, but that's a tale for another day).

Transitioning from an entrepreneur to a public servant was a mixed bag. On one side, it was a seamless shift, but on the other, it was an abrupt wake-up call. Suddenly, my family had to reassess our lifestyle, recalibrate our spending habits, and seriously reconsider our financial planning due to a decrease in income. It forced us to confront decisions we'd previously taken for granted.

During this phase, a men's group I belonged to planned a weekend trip to Chicago. The cost was beyond my means at that point. Upon discovering that I was bowing out because of the costs, my friends in the group divided the trip expenses among themselves so I could join. Initially, I resisted—feeling uncomfortable accepting their generosity, adamant about not being a charity case. Their kindness, while well-intended, made me feel diminished.

One of the group members took me aside after my initial refusal and shared a profound insight: "Paul, you need to learn the art of being a cheerful receiver. You've been a cheerful giver, but in this chapter of your life, it's time to learn how to receive." A cheerful receiver—what a novel concept! It reshaped my perspective on receiving generosity, transforming my understanding of how it blesses both the giver and the receiver.

Scripture is rich with stories of individuals graciously accepting gifts, not rejecting them out of a sense of unworthiness. Take the ultimate gift: Jesus' sacrifice on the cross. It's a profound reminder that we can't earn it—we simply receive it with gratitude and open hearts. Learning to be a grateful receiver, I realized, is as much a virtue as being a cheerful giver.

> **Quotable:** "Gracious acceptance is an art—an art which most never bother to cultivate. We think that we have to learn how to give, but we forget about accepting things, which can be much harder than giving ... Accepting another person's gift is allowing him to express his feelings for you" (Alexander McCall Smith).

> **What does scripture say?** "Every good gift and every perfect gift is from above, coming down from the Father of lights, with whom there is no variation or shadow due to change" (James 1:17).

Reflection: In what areas of your life do you need to become a better receiver?

Take time to reflect on your notes from last week. What worked and what didn't?

_____

_____

_____

_____

_____

What is one goal I want to be intentional about accomplishing this week?

_____

_____

_____

_____

What is one relationship I am going to focus on this week?

_____

_____

_____

_____

What is one thing I can do this week to better my physical and/or mental health?

_____

_____

_____

_____

What am I grateful for in my life right now?

_____

_____

_____

_____

Spend time in prayer following the P.A.T.H. (Praise, Admit, Thank, Help).

ACCEPTANCE VS. CELEBRATION

I n our complex and diverse world, clashes over beliefs and values are commonplace. We're nudged constantly to pick sides on cultural and societal issues, oftentimes with an urging by the media and those around us to champion causes even when they clash with our personal convictions.

As a public servant, I faced a similar dilemma on a regular basis. There was an expectation by some in my community to endorse perspectives that contradicted my Christian values, all in the name of representing a community with a variety of viewpoints. Afterall, I was a mayor of a broad and growing community, so many assumed my personal views needed to be equally as broad. But did my role as mayor truly require me to compromise my personal beliefs in order to effectively serve those around me?

Looking to Jesus' example, he masterfully balanced acceptance without necessarily celebrating actions contrary to his faith. In John 8, when confronted with a woman caught in adultery, he didn't endorse her actions but extended empathy and grace, urging her toward a better path ("Go, and sin no more"). It's a nuanced approach that modern society often struggles to grasp and, if not balanced with empathy, can easily be viewed as condemnation.

Amid the culture wars of the day, it's essential for Christians to speak truth with love, navigating the fine line of accepting those around us as children of God while not endorsing actions that contradict one's own Christian beliefs. It's about embracing empathy without necessarily celebrating behaviors that run against the grain of our faith—mirroring the delicate balance Jesus demonstrated during his ministry on earth.

> **Quotable:** "The only way to speak the truth is to speak lovingly" (Henry David Thoreau).

> **What does scripture say?** "Jesus straightened up and asked her, 'Woman, where are they? Has no one condemned you?' 'No one, sir,' she said. 'Then neither do I condemn you,' Jesus declared. 'Go now and leave your life of sin'" (John 8:10-11).

> **Reflection:** What current events/issues do you struggle with in accepting the views of others while not condemning them? How would Jesus approach this issue with which you are wrestling?

Take time to reflect on your notes from last week. What worked and what didn't?

_____

_____

_____

_____

_____

What is one goal I want to be intentional about accomplishing this week?

_____

_____

_____

_____

_____

What is one relationship I am going to focus on this week?

_____

_____

_____

_____

What is one thing I can do this week to better my physical and/or mental health?

_____

_____

_____

_____

_____

What am I grateful for in my life right now?

_____

_____

_____

_____

_____

Spend time in prayer following the P.A.T.H. (Praise, Admit, Thank, Help).

WEEK 30

LISTENING WELL

I n the realm of public service, feedback becomes a steady companion—whether solicited or not. It arrives via letters, meetings, social media, newspaper columns, and presents a myriad of opinions both to and about elected leaders. Afterall, it's called "public" service for a reason—the work and those we work for are very public!

At the onset of my tenure as mayor, I'll admit that the feedback often provoked frustration for me. Some messages and very public feedback contained inaccuracies, assumptions, or even personal attacks that stirred my desire to retaliate and set the record straight. In my prior private sector experience, such unprofessional behavior and attacks wouldn't have been tolerated, so why should they be in this job, I thought. The temptation to "hit back" was very strong.

Then came a piece of advice from a good friend: buried within most negative feedback often lies a nugget of truth, if you're willing to look for it. It's a concept that's tough to embrace initially, but one that proved valid. I honed my skill not just in listening but in truly hearing people out (And there's a significant difference between listening and hearing).

Whenever I encountered challenging remarks, I started asking, "Is there a grain of truth in this criticism, and what can I learn from it?" Yet, let's not ignore the fact that some negative words are solely meant to cause harm—a separate challenge that demands a different approach.

Learning from our sternest critics can be a valuable means to sharpen our abilities and who we are as individuals. Instead of immediately adopting a defensive stance when faced with unfavorable feedback, I've found that examining its source and content often leads to insightful revelations about both the source and myself.

So, the next time you encounter less-than-rosy feedback, consider diving deeper into its core rather than just brushing it off. You'll be astounded by the lessons you unearth—about the feedback giver and, more importantly, about yourself.

> **Quotable:** "Examine what is said and not who speaks" (African proverb).

> **What does scripture say?** "The way of a fool is right in his own eyes, but a wise one listens to advice" (Proverbs 12:15).

> **Reflection:** Think about some criticism you have received recently. How did you react? In examining it, is there truth to what was shared?

Take time to reflect on your notes from last week. What worked and what didn't?

_____

_____

_____

_____

_____

What is one goal I want to be intentional about accomplishing this week?

_____

_____

_____

_____

_____

What is one relationship I am going to focus on this week?

_____

_____

_____

_____

_____

_____

What is one thing I can do this week to better my physical and/or mental health?

_____

_____

_____

_____

_____

What am I grateful for in my life right now?

_____

_____

_____

_____

Spend time in prayer following the P.A.T.H. (Praise, Admit, Thank, Help).

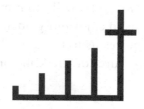

A KINGDOM RETIREMENT PLAN

The American dream, for decades, has promised us the freedoms and opportunities to navigate our personal and professional journeys, culminating in the ability to eventually retire and live a life on our terms. This cultural view of retirement has caused many to view work merely as a means to an end—a financial buildup to bid adieu to employment and welcome a life of leisure. This vision holds promise, but does it align with what Scripture asks of us?

While prudent financial planning and ensuring sustained service to the Lord well into our senior years are vital, the prevalent cultural concept of retirement often strays from biblical principles. In fact, Scripture warns against accumulating wealth solely for personal gain (Luke 12:16-21).

So, how should believers approach retirement? Considering it a chapter of financial freedom might distance us from the dependence we ought to have on God. We're called to rely on Him for our daily bread. When we start assuming control of our future entirely and put our hope and trust into a 401K, we start to drift from our reliance on God, who will often nudge us back toward Him. Does God want us to enjoy our golden years? Of course He does. But God also requires us to finish well and to use our gifts of time, talent, and treasure for the kingdom through our final day on earth.

Retirement, in a biblical sense, should signify a shift toward a new chapter of "kingdom usefulness" rather than a point where we disengage from work to focus solely on self-investment. This perspective challenges the prevalent societal notion of "you've earned it," yet it's the paradigm God invites us to embrace during the retirement chapter of our earthly journey.

> **Quotable:** "Age is not all decay; it is the ripening, the swelling, of the fresh life within, that withers and bursts the husk" (George Macdonald).

> **What does scripture say?** "Even until your old age, I am the one, and I'll carry you even until your gray hairs come. It is I who have created, and I who will carry, and it is I who will bear and save" (Isaiah 46:4-5).

> **Reflection:** When you think ahead to retirement, what does that look like for you? In thinking about your own views of finances and retirement, do they include a trust and reliance on God?

Take time to reflect on your notes from last week. What worked and what didn't?

_____

_____

_____

_____

_____

What is one goal I want to be intentional about accomplishing this week?

_____

_____

_____

_____

_____

What is one relationship I am going to focus on this week?

_____

_____

_____

_____

_____

What is one thing I can do this week to better my physical and/or mental health?

_____

_____

_____

_____

_____

What am I grateful for in my life right now?

_____

_____

_____

_____

_____

Spend time in prayer following the P.A.T.H. (Praise, Admit, Thank, Help).

WEEK 32

HELPFUL HABITS

The lives of remarkable leaders often unveil a common thread: their dedication to cultivating positive daily habits. Take a closer look, and you'll find Bill Gates prioritizing daily meditation, Winston Churchill indulging in regular catnaps, Arnold Schwarzenegger's unwavering commitment to daily workouts, and Tim Cook's 4:00 AM wake-up ritual. If you have leaders in your inner circle whom you admire what their daily habits are, I am sure you will find some similar themes.

When you assess your aspirations and who you aim to become, identifying the essential habits you need to form becomes pivotal to attaining your goals. Personally, I've anchored my day with three non-negotiable habits: an early rise, morning exercise, and dedicated time for devotions and prayer. These rituals grant me the gift of personal reflection, physical well-being, and spiritual nourishment—often before the sun is even up. They epitomize vital traits every leader should nurture, and devoting the initial hours of each day to these habits fuels me to tackle challenges head-on as the day unfolds.

One of my admired voices in leadership development, Craig Groeschel, wisely notes, "Leaders do the small things that no one sees to get the results that everyone wants." I love the poignant truth in this statement. In our world fixated on instant results, we often overlook the grind, the habitual routines, and the consistent effort invested over time to achieve success. However, you would be hard-pressed to find an established and successful leader who has not mastered the art of creating small, effective habits.

Positive habit forming is all about repetition, unwavering consistency, and tweaking the formula continually as life and goals evolve. In my experience, this formula remains the bedrock of enduring leadership success.

> **Quotable:** "Habit is the intersection of knowledge (what to do), skill (how to do), and desire (want to do)" (Stephen R. Covey).

> **What does scripture say**? "Let your eyes look straight ahead; fix your gaze directly before you. Give careful thought to the paths for your feet and be steadfast in all your ways" (Proverbs 4:25-26).

> **Reflection:** What habits do you currently have that need correcting? Are there new habits you need to form in order to become the person God intended you to be?

Take time to reflect on your notes from last week. What worked and what didn't?

_____

_____

_____

_____

_____

What is one goal I want to be intentional about accomplishing this week?

_____

_____

_____

_____

_____

What is one relationship I am going to focus on this week?

_____

_____

_____

_____

What is one thing I can do this week to better my physical and/or mental health?

_____

_____

_____

_____

_____

What am I grateful for in my life right now?

_____

_____

_____

_____

Spend time in prayer following the P.A.T.H. (Praise, Admit, Thank, Help).

PAUL TENHAKEN

WEEK 33

DEALING WITH ANXIOUSNESS

According to the U.S. Census Bureau Household Pulse Survey, nearly one-third of adults (32.3%) reported anxiety and depression symptoms in 2023. In an era where constant connectivity to television, social media, and a barrage of negative news inundates us on a daily basis, it's no wonder anxiety holds so many Americans in its grip.

Personally, I'm no stranger to grappling with anxiety. The ceaseless demands of my role in public service, coupled with mounting community expectations, often foster feelings of doubt, worry, and unease in my daily life. I'd hazard a guess that a majority of executives and senior leaders face similar struggles at some point in their careers. As responsibilities increase, so do expectations, and with increased expectations comes the corresponding anxiety around performance.

The peak of my anxiety came in 2020 amid the trials of the COVID-19 pandemic. The relentless pressure across all fronts of pandemic management became almost unbearable as the pandemic wore on. My sleep suffered, my weight plummeted, and my mental well-being took a significant blow. It became clear that relying solely on my own strengths and capabilities to navigate the pandemic's challenges would be woefully insufficient. It was then that I leaned into God and my faith more than ever before. I had painfully honest conversations with God, I completely surrendered the situation to Him, fully facing my inadequacies in leading through an unwinnable situation.

Dealing with anxiety or depression is not something Christians should shy away from or feel ashamed to discuss. It's a signal that we're confronting burdens beyond our individual capacity, a moment when we must learn to lean on our friends, family, and faith. There's no shame in acknowledging those chapters when anxiety can grip your life. God offers the ultimate remedy and peace, if only we humbly surrender and accept it.

> **Quotable:** "The more you pray, the less you'll panic. The more you worship, the less you worry. You'll feel more patient and less pressured." (Rick Warren).

> **What does scripture say?** ""Be anxious for nothing, but in everything by prayer and supplication, with thanksgiving, let your requests be made known to God; and the peace of God, which surpasses all understanding, will guard your hearts and minds through Christ Jesus" (Philippians 4:6-7).

> **Reflection:** What areas of your life are currently causing you anxiety? Lift them up to God in prayer today and surrender.

Take time to reflect on your notes from last week. What worked and what didn't?

_____

_____

_____

_____

_____

What is one goal I want to be intentional about accomplishing this week?

_____

_____

_____

_____

What is one relationship I am going to focus on this week?

_____

_____

_____

_____

_____

What is one thing I can do this week to better my physical and/or mental health?

_____

_____

_____

_____

_____

What am I grateful for in my life right now?

_____

_____

_____

_____

_____

Spend time in prayer following the P.A.T.H. (Praise, Admit, Thank, Help).

WEEK 34

DISCERNING
GOD'S WILL

D o you ever encounter those individuals who seem to have a direct hotline to God? They casually mention, "God spoke to me" or "God made it crystal clear to me" when discussing life-altering decisions they've made. I'll admit I've felt a twinge of envy toward those who seemingly discern God's will far more easily than I seem to.

In 2015, I was riding high on the waves of entrepreneurship, thoroughly enjoying steering the marketing firm I had founded. The business was scaling rapidly, the work was invigorating, and I eagerly anticipated Mondays to dive into the career path I believed God had laid before me. However, that year, I sensed a nudge from God, a subtle questioning of whether my current career was meant to be a lifelong journey. Restlessness crept in, hinting that there might be more for me, a deeper way to serve the kingdom than my entrepreneurial pursuits allowed.

Regular prayer became my compass as I sought God's guidance for my career. I sought counsel from trusted friends in my inner circle. I dove into intense Bible studies, hoping for a glimpse of God's plan. Eventually, through these channels and more, it became apparent that God was leading me to untangle myself from the company—something that had become my identity—and explore a new arena of service. Surprisingly, that path led me to become the mayor of South Dakota's largest city, a role I was ill-equipped and underprepared for. Yet, I plunged into it, trusting that "He who calls you to it will get you through it."

Discerning God's will demands patience, surrender, and, often, a willingness to step out of our comfort zones. Before you make significant life decisions—be it a major purchase, a career shift, or the next chapter for your family—take it to the Lord in prayer. Immerse yourself in Scripture. Open up the issue to those closest to you. God employs various means to guide us in discerning His will, and when we heed that guidance, you will find that His will is always perfect.

> **Quotable:** "If you yourself do not cut the lines that tie you to the dock, God will have to use a storm to sever them and to send you out to sea. You have to get out past the harbor into the great depths of God and begin to know things for yourself…begin to have spiritual discernment. Beware of paying attention or going back to what you once were, when God wants you to be something that you have never been" (Oswald Chambers).

> **What does scripture say?** "So now, go. I am sending you to Pharaoh to bring my people the Israelites out of Egypt." But Moses said to God, "Who am I that I

PAUL TENHAKEN

should go to Pharaoh and bring the Israelites out of Egypt?" And God said, "I will be with you" (Exodus 3:10-12a).

Reflection: In what area of your life are you currently relying on your own wisdom instead of seeking God for discernment? What major decision are you currently facing? How will you bring God into the decision-making process?

Take time to reflect on your notes from last week. What worked and what didn't?

_____

_____

_____

_____

_____

_____

What is one goal I want to be intentional about accomplishing this week?

_____

_____

_____

_____

_____

_____

What is one relationship I am going to focus on this week?

_____

_____

_____

_____

What is one thing I can do this week to better my physical and/or mental health?

_____

_____

_____

_____

_____

What am I grateful for in my life right now?

_____

_____

_____

_____

_____

Spend time in prayer following the P.A.T.H. (Praise, Admit, Thank, Help).

CHOOSING TO END IN ORDER TO BEGIN

Endings have long been associated with finality—an unmistakable conclusion. A movie concludes, a vacation wraps up, a school year ends, and careers reach their closing chapters. There's a sense of closure, transitioning these experiences into memories. However, my perspective on endings has recently evolved—I now see them as gateways to new beginnings, the closure of one chapter allowing a fresh chapter to unfold. While bidding farewell to a chapter can be bittersweet or challenging, often, our lives and the purpose that God intends for us can only commence once we close that chapter.

In his book "Necessary Endings," Henry Cloud frames it powerfully: "Getting to the next level always requires ending something, leaving it behind, and moving on. Growth itself demands that we move on. Without the ability to end things, people stay stuck, never becoming who they are meant to be, never accomplishing all that their talents and abilities should afford them."

I vividly recall a former colleague whose constant negativity left me feeling drained, deflated, and often angry. It reached a point where I had to distance myself, minimizing communication unless absolutely necessary. I prayed for them, wishing happiness in their life, but I realized I didn't need to expose myself to their negativity. Cutting ties led me to a new phase in my work, one where I found greater joy and contentment simply by ending a toxic relationship. It was, as Henry Cloud states, a necessary ending.

Among the most challenging endings are those concerning relationships. Whether a painful divorce, a toxic friendship, or a family member entangled in drama, deciding to conclude these relationships in search of new beginnings can be emotionally taxing. Yet, remaining involved in draining, negative relationships hampers our growth. We'll never fully embrace the person God intends us to be if we remain tethered to relationships that continually drag us down. Sometimes, we must choose an ending in order to find a new beginning.

> **Quotable:** "Great is the art of beginning, but greater is the art of ending" (Henry Wadsworth Longfellow).

> **What does scripture say?** "There is a time for everything, and a season for every activity under the heavens" (Ecclesiastes 3:1).

> **Reflection:** Is there a relationship in your life that needs to be ended in order for you to move forward in God's plan for your life?

Take time to reflect on your notes from last week. What worked and what didn't?

_____

_____

_____

_____

_____

What is one goal I want to be intentional about accomplishing this week?

_____

_____

_____

_____

_____

What is one relationship I am going to focus on this week?

_____

_____

_____

_____

_____

What is one thing I can do this week to better my physical and/or mental health?

_____

_____

_____

_____

_____

What am I grateful for in my life right now?

_____

_____

_____

_____

_____

Spend time in prayer following the P.A.T.H. (Praise, Admit, Thank, Help).

WEEK 36

HOW MUCH IS ENOUGH?

They say money is a necessity in life but holds no meaning in death. We devote much of our lives to accumulating wealth, only to discover that the fulfillment society promises through riches is an illusion. So, what should we do with our money? Or, more importantly, what should we do with the resources God has entrusted us with?

Many of us are blessed with careers that sustain us, enabling us to meet our needs and, with prudence, enjoy some discretionary spending. Like a parent revels in their child's joy while unwrapping and relishing a gift, God delights in witnessing our enjoyment of material blessings from the financial provisions He grants. But where does one draw the line? Is having a functional car sufficient, or do we strive for a luxurious sports car? Is a roof over our heads satisfactory, or should it be the most extravagant house in the neighborhood? And if so, is there anything wrong in that pursuit?

These are questions I've grappled with over the years, especially when investing in material possessions or planning nice vacations with my family. Is this how God intends for me to use His resources? Could the funds for my new deck be better utilized supporting missionaries abroad? Is my decade-old car truly inadequate when considering those who have never even owned a vehicle?

These dilemmas are challenging, and there isn't a one-size-fits-all solution. I believe each person should pray, reflect, and study this issue, aligning their actions with what feels right for their family and their relationship with God. What's suitable for one might not be fitting for another, but nurturing a personal connection with God in how you handle your finances is what He desires. There will always be someone with a grander home, a fatter bank account, or finer possessions. Finding contentment in the blessings God has bestowed upon you, without comparison to others, will bring profound peace and guide you in recognizing when "enough" truly is enough.

> **Quotable:** "Men lose all the material things they leave behind them in this world, but they carry with them the reward of their charity and the alms they give. For these, they will receive from the Lord the reward and recompense they deserve" (Francis of Assisi).

> **What does scripture say?** "Then he said to them, 'Watch out! Be on your guard against all kinds of greed; life does not consist in an abundance of possessions'" (Luke 12:15).

Reflection: Are there areas of your life where you struggle with contentment and feeling like you have enough? What can you do to find peace in how God has blessed you materially?

Take time to reflect on your notes from last week. What worked and what didn't?

_____

_____

_____

_____

_____

What is one goal I want to be intentional about accomplishing this week?

_____

_____

_____

_____

_____

What is one relationship I am going to focus on this week?

_____

_____

_____

_____

_____

What is one thing I can do this week to better my physical and/or mental health?

_____

_____

_____

_____

_____

What am I grateful for in my life right now?

_____

_____

_____

_____

Spend time in prayer following the P.A.T.H. (Praise, Admit, Thank, Help).

WEEK 37

WITNESSING AT WORK

The average person invests over 90,000 hours at work throughout their lifetime—a staggering one-third of their entire existence! When sleep, consuming another third of our lives, is excluded, it becomes clear that work claims more time in our lives than any other activity.

Given the immense role that work plays, it's wise to explore how our faith and work intersect. I often hear the phrase "Sunday into Monday," which prompts us to consider how we carry the lessons and rhythms of Sunday into our workweek on Monday. In our present time, the fear of offending people around us can often stifle openness about our faith in Christ and our true selves at work. So, how can we be more bold in our faith at work?

Here are three ways believers can manifest their faith in the workplace while honoring the diverse beliefs and perspectives of their colleagues:

Be Kind. Simple as it sounds, displaying the love of Christ begins with genuine care and kindness toward others. Engage with empathy. Demonstrate your love through actions, especially toward those who may be challenging to love. Being kind to everyone, even when it's difficult, speaks volumes about your faith.

Emulate Christ. Jesus provided us an incredible example to follow in demonstrating love to those around us each day. Every interaction, conversation, and connection with people is an opportunity to reflect Christ's love through our words and actions.

Be Ready to Share. Always be prepared to explain why you have a daily sense of joy, contagious energy, and a perspective that others might find unconventional. Be open to discussing your faith and the reasons behind your demeanor. As your light shines brightly, opportunities to share your beliefs and hope in Jesus Christ will naturally arise.

When we perceive work as a platform for ministry rather than merely a job or a means to earn money, it transforms our perspective. It offers us the chance to serve God through our vocations, viewing work as an opportunity to love and impact people positively.

Quotable: "Be a good witness by the way you live. The way we live is often more convincing than the words we say" (Billy Graham).

What does scripture say? "But the fruit of the Spirit is love, joy, peace, forbearance, kindness, goodness, faithfulness and self-control. Against such things there is no law" (Galatians 5:22-23).

Reflection: Are there areas of your life where you struggle with contentment and feeling like you have enough? What can you do to find peace in how God has blessed you materially?

Take time to reflect on your notes from last week. What worked and what didn't?

_____

_____

_____

_____

_____

_____

What is one goal I want to be intentional about accomplishing this week?

_____

_____

_____

_____

_____

_____

What is one relationship I am going to focus on this week?

_____

_____

_____

_____

_____

What is one thing I can do this week to better my physical and/or mental health?

_____

_____

_____

_____

_____

What am I grateful for in my life right now?

_____

_____

_____

_____

_____

Spend time in prayer following the P.A.T.H. (Praise, Admit, Thank, Help.

WEEK 38

ASSUMING POSITIVE INTENT

Navigating public service often means grappling with critics. In my opinion, it's one of the hardest parts of being an elected official. Every decision made or stance taken seems to draw opposition, evolving from healthy disagreement to a level of anger and hostility that's becoming all too common these days.

I vividly recall a situation involving a longtime friend and respected community member. We had a history long before my public service days, a bond that seemed to fracture when we found ourselves on opposing sides of an issue after I got into office. What saddened me was how quickly things turned personal, and words became cutting over what I believe were quite minor items. I had to remind my friend that beneath the disagreement, I was still the person he'd known for many years despite my new community role, and our differences on this particular matter shouldn't overshadow that.

Assuming positive intent when faced with disagreements is a powerful approach. It's unlikely any leader wakes up in the morning, looks in the mirror, and says, "I wonder how I can intentionally upset people today?" Whether it's someone in a position of authority or influence or a friend or family member, approaching disputes with a presumption of positive intent can lead to a more composed and empathetic dialogue, even if viewpoints diverge.

Next time you find yourself getting heated over a diverging opinion or perceived wrongdoing with someone in your circle, take a step back. Try to view them through a lens of positive intent. While you may not reach an agreement, this perspective shift often leads to a better understanding, fostering more productive discussions despite the differences.

> **Quotable:** "Believe in the goodness of all people. Assume positive intent and be quick to forgive mistakes" (Mary Frances Winters).

> **What does scripture say?** "Love never gives up, never loses faith, is always hopeful, and endures through every circumstance" (I Corinthians 13:7).

> **Reflection:** Are there people in your life who you are harboring anger or frustration toward because of a perceived wrongdoing? How does assuming positive intent in how they've wronged you change your perspective?

Take time to reflect on your notes from last week. What worked and what didn't?

_____

_____

_____

_____

_____

What is one goal I want to be intentional about accomplishing this week?

_____

_____

_____

_____

_____

What is one relationship I am going to focus on this week?

_____

_____

_____

_____

What is one thing I can do this week to better my physical and/or mental health?

_____

_____

_____

_____

_____

What am I grateful for in my life right now?

_____

_____

_____

_____

Spend time in prayer following the P.A.T.H. (Praise, Admit, Thank, Help).

FEED YOUR MIND

I n today's hyper-connected world, our attention is a battleground, largely due to the soaring prevalence of smartphones. According to a recent 2023 study by Reviews.org, people, on average, check their phones 144 times a day, engaging in various activities, from emails to social media, gaming, video streaming, and more. However, while some of this digital consumption might be productive, a considerable chunk of screen time involves content that isn't necessarily beneficial for our mental well-being.

Consider your mind as you would your body. Just as your body needs balanced nutrition for optimal performance, your mind requires healthy input to function at its best. Continuous consumption of social media, mindless videos, and games can be likened to "junk food" for the mind. Occasional indulgence isn't harmful, but a steady diet of these digital distractions can have adverse effects.

Similarly, the 24/7 news cycle we live in inundates us with a constant stream of often negative information. Unlike the days when morning newspapers and nightly news updates sufficed, today's continuous news bombardment can subtly shape our mindset toward the negative. Staying informed is crucial, but constantly exposing ourselves to negative news can subconsciously alter our perspectives.

I abide by the principle of moderation in all aspects of life, including digital media and news consumption. Setting limits on how much and where we engage with digital content is essential. By controlling what we feed our minds, we create space for spiritual growth, allowing God's Word to influence and guide our lives instead of relying solely on screens and external sources.

> **Quotable:** "Deliberately feed your mind the good, the pure, the powerful and the positive" (Zig Ziglar).

> **What does scripture say?** "More than anything you guard, protect your mind, for life flows from it. Have nothing to do with a corrupt mouth; keep devious lips far from you. Focus your eyes straight ahead; keep your gaze on what is in front of you. Watch your feet on the way, and all your paths will be secure" (Proverbs 4:23-27).

> **Reflection:** How can you better protect your mind and feed it in a healthy way? What is one tangible change you will make in this area?

Take time to reflect on your notes from last week. What worked and what didn't?

_____

_____

_____

What is one goal I want to be intentional about accomplishing this week?

_____

_____

_____

_____

_____

What is one relationship I am going to focus on this week?

_____

_____

_____

_____

What is one thing I can do this week to better my physical and/or mental health?

_____

_____

_____

_____

_____

What am I grateful for in my life right now?

_____

_____

_____

_____

Spend time in prayer following the P.A.T.H. (Praise, Admit, Thank, Help).

QUARTER THREE CHECK-IN

Your year is now three-quarters over, and you have been following *The Code of Contentment* for nine months. Congratulations! Take time now to look back over your journaling from the past three months. When you've finished doing that, review the following questions:

How am I doing with the goals I have set this past quarter? Where am I succeeding, and where am I failing?

_____

_____

_____

_____

_____

_____

What have been my biggest wins with the relationships I have focused on? What relationships do I need to improve?

_____

_____

_____

_____

_____

Being honest with myself, how do I feel about my physical and mental health right now? Have I made an impact on my overall wellness in the last quarter?

_____

_____

_____

_____

_____

Thinking about the last three months, what areas of my life am I most thankful for?

_____

_____

_____

_____

_____

PAUL TENHAKEN

WHAT'S IN YOUR BOX?

Prioritization is an ongoing challenge in our fast-paced lives and personally, is something I have struggled with for many years. Every day, we juggle numerous aspects of life—work, family, friends, hobbies, deadlines, kids' activities, faith, and more. Finding equilibrium among these demands often feels like a high-wire act in a circus.

There are a multitude of resources out there, from self-help books to apps on our phones, that attempt to guide us in compartmentalizing our lives efficiently. A simple search for "prioritizing" in the book section on Amazon.com will return thousands of results on books that offer strategies to manage time and talents, aiming to maximize our priorities and ensure we become the best versions of ourselves.

A popular concept in prioritization books encourages the reader to ask, "What's in your box?" It's a simple yet powerful inquiry about our life's primary focus. Imagine your life as a box, allowing room for just one priority. While we obviously have many complicated elements to our lives, the box concept pushes us to focus on the main thing. If it's your career, everything else, including faith and family, becomes secondary. The box can only hold one thing, and our life's judgment hinges on what we put inside.

For those of faith, the ideal answer should be clear—God should be in our box. However, honest introspection often reveals a disparity between what we know needs to be our main priority and what our actions reflect. I, too, grapple with this dichotomy. Despite claiming God is my priority, I sometimes fall short in living out that belief throughout my day.

Reflect today on what occupies your box, and be ruthlessly honest with yourself. If you're unsatisfied with the answer, how will you pivot to align your actions with your priorities?

> **Quotable:** "The main thing is to keep the main thing the main thing" (Stephen Covey).

> **What does scripture say?** "In everything you do, put God first, and he will direct you and crown your efforts with success" (Proverbs 3:6).

> **Reflection:** Does your life accurately reflect what you feel is in your box? What distractions in your life must you remove in order to keep the main thing, the main thing?

Take time to reflect on your notes from last week. What worked and what didn't?

_____

_____

_____

_____

_____

What is one goal I want to be intentional about accomplishing this week?

_____

_____

_____

_____

_____

What is one relationship I am going to focus on this week?

_____

_____

_____

_____

_____

What is one thing I can do this week to better my physical and/or mental health?

_____

_____

_____

_____

_____

What am I grateful for in my life right now?

_____

_____

_____

_____

_____

Spend time in prayer following the P.A.T.H. (Praise, Admit, Thank, Help).

THE RAT RACE REALITY

The term "rat race" has a storied history, tracing back to its origins in aviation training in the 1930s and later morphing into a phrase to describe the competitive struggles of work life from the mid-twentieth century onward. It's emblematic of the challenges we face daily in our professional lives.

In the hustle and bustle of our work, it's easy to lose sight of the bigger picture: just like our lives, work will eventually come to an end. This fact might seem obvious, yet amidst the daily grind, it's often overlooked. I've witnessed individuals sacrifice fundamental aspects of their lives—marriages, health, friendships, and faith—all in pursuit of staying ahead in this relentless race. It becomes a pursuit where the costs outweigh the rewards if not viewed with proper perspective.

Ecclesiastes, authored by King Solomon, resonates profoundly with me. Solomon, a figure who seemingly possessed everything one could desire, reflects on life's follies in a world-worn tone. Despite his access to wisdom, pleasure, and substantial resources, his reflection reveals a poignant regret, guiding us toward a simpler life in alignment with God's direction. He initiates this contemplation by asking, "What do people gain from all their labors at which they toil under the sun? Generations come and generations go, but the earth remains forever" (Ecclesiastes 1:3-4).

Work indeed stands as a blessing from God, a means through which we honor Him. However, it's crucial to keep its role in our lives in perspective. The annals of history are replete with the stories of "successful" individuals who excelled in the rat race but faltered in their spiritual and personal lives. For Christians, it's imperative to balance career pursuits with the understanding that Solomon concluded at the end of his life: "Fear God and obey His commands, for this is everyone's duty. God will judge us for everything we do, including every secret thing, whether good or bad" (Ecclesiastes 12:13-14).

> **Quotable:** "Jesus is the only significance. Beside Jesus nothing has any significance. He alone matters" (Dietrich Bonhoeffer).

> **What does scripture say?** "And I know that whatever God does is final. Nothing can be added to it or taken from it. God's purpose is that people should fear him" (Ecclesiastes 3:14).

> **Reflection:** Are your career pursuits driven by the desire for personal gain or the desire to advance the kingdom of God?

Take time to reflect on your notes from last week. What worked and what didn't?

_____

_____

_____

_____

_____

What is one goal I want to be intentional about accomplishing this week?

_____

_____

_____

_____

_____

What is one relationship I am going to focus on this week?

_____

_____

_____

_____

_____

_____

What is one thing I can do this week to better my physical and/or mental health?

_____

_____

_____

_____

_____

What am I grateful for in my life right now?

_____

_____

_____

_____

_____

Spend time in prayer following the P.A.T.H. (Praise, Admit, Thank, Help).

WEEK 42

THE BIBLICAL CALLING TO MENTOR

Over my years of public service, I've seen far too many people put faith in government as the solution to all societal challenges. While elected leaders and government do have responsibilities to foster solutions, I've never wholly subscribed to the belief that they are the sole solution. Throughout my tenure as mayor, addressing complex issues like homelessness, juvenile crime, mental health struggles, and addiction has been a significant part of my focus. Despite the allocation of substantial resources, millions of dollars, and numerous programs, quantifiable progress can sometimes feel elusive in some of these problem areas.

There's an old adage: "Just because you can't do everything doesn't mean you shouldn't do something." Often, when confronted with the magnitude of a complex problem, it seems futile that any single individual can make any meaningful impact. Yet, this perspective is rooted in our culture of immediate gratification—where we demand instant results to even the most challenging problems. Realizing that profound societal issues demand consistent, incremental efforts helps us uncover more pragmatic solutions.

Mentorship has always stood out to me as a profound, biblical means to influence our world. It's easy to point fingers at the challenges around us, but true change happens when we engage directly. Rolling up our sleeves might mean walking alongside someone battling addiction, supporting a single parent with child care, or aiding a former inmate in securing employment. Virtually every individual on this planet can benefit from a deliberate, one-on-one relationship with a mentor or accountability partner. Those relationships—one by one—can slowly add up to have an impact at scale.

The next time you're compelled to highlight societal issues, ask yourself how you're actively becoming the change you want to see by engaging in mentorship. You'll discover that the personal rewards you gain from a mentoring relationship will often outweigh the perceived benefits you offer your mentee. Consider investing in someone today.

> **Quotable:** "You cannot teach a man anything. You can only help him discover it within himself" (Galileo Galilei).

> **What does scripture say?** "Be shepherds of God's flock that is under your care, watching over them—not because you must, but because you are willing, as God wants you to be; not pursuing dishonest gain, but eager to serve; not lording it over those entrusted to you, but being examples to the flock" (1 Peter 5:2-3).

Reflection: Take time to think about people who have invested in and mentored you over the years. Who is God nudging you toward a mentoring relationship with? How will you take the first step in that effort this week?

Take time to reflect on your notes from last week. What worked and what didn't?

_____

_____

_____

_____

_____

What is one goal I want to be intentional about accomplishing this week?

_____

_____

_____

_____

_____

What is one relationship I am going to focus on this week?

_____

_____

_____

_____

_____

What is one thing I can do this week to better my physical and/or mental health?

_____

_____

_____

_____

_____

What am I grateful for in my life right now?

_____

_____

_____

_____

_____

Spend time in prayer following the P.A.T.H. (Praise, Admit, Thank, Help).

PAUL TENHAKEN

A GOAL OR A WISH?

'm passionate about setting and achieving goals. Every year, I eagerly sketch out a plan encompassing both personal aspirations and professional milestones I hope to conquer. These ambitions span a wide spectrum, ranging from competing in triathlons to curating memorable experiences for my kids or venturing into the entrepreneurial realm with a new business venture. Although I'm not particularly drawn to New Year's resolutions, I firmly believe in cataloging ambitions and charting a clear pathway to attaining them—and not just in January.

"A goal without a plan is just a wish" has always been a resonating phrase for me. It emphasizes the importance of not just setting goals but constructing a blueprint or strategy to navigate toward them. Without a structured approach, goals often linger unfulfilled. So, how do I ensure my aspirations materialize rather than remain a list of unaccomplished dreams? Here are three strategies that have significantly elevated my personal and professional goal-setting:

Set realistic yet ambitious goals: Striking a balance between ambition and practicality is paramount. It's crucial to be aware of your current position and capabilities while daring to dream big. I firmly believe it's better to aim high and slightly miss than to set the bar too low and hit it effortlessly.

Share your goals with a level of public commitment: While not necessarily broadcasting to the entire world, sharing your ambitions with a trusted circle or a wider network creates an inherent sense of accountability. This commitment keeps me focused and driven toward achieving my objectives.

Break down goals into manageable sub-goals: Achieving significant milestones is a gradual process. Just as a marathon doesn't happen overnight, breaking down larger goals into smaller, achievable targets ensures steady progress and prevents feeling overwhelmed by the magnitude of the primary goal.

Individuals who have accomplished great feats in life are often intentional about setting and pursuing goals. Allowing life to simply unfold without a clear vision can limit one's potential. Realistic goal-setting is about embracing challenges, realizing potential, and expanding horizons beyond your own perceived limits.

> **Quotable:** "If you set goals and go after them with all the determination you can muster, your gifts will take you places that will amaze you" (Les Brown).

> **What does scripture say?** "The plans of the diligent lead to profit as surely as haste leads to poverty" (Proverbs 21:5).

> **Reflection:** In what areas of your life do you need to set goals in order to achieve God's plan He has for you? What goals have you set over the years but never seem to accomplish, and how can you change that?

Take time to reflect on your notes from last week. What worked and what didn't?

_____

_____

_____

_____

_____

What is one goal I want to be intentional about accomplishing this week?

_____

_____

_____

_____

_____

What is one relationship I am going to focus on this week?

_____

_____

_____

_____

_____

_____

What is one thing I can do this week to better my physical and/or mental health?

_____

_____

_____

_____

_____

What am I grateful for in my life right now?

_____

_____

_____

_____

_____

Spend time in prayer following the P.A.T.H. (Praise, Admit, Thank, Help).

WEEK 44

THE FREEDOM
OF APOLOGY

"Happy Days" was a classic TV show that I would watch when I was a child, and the iconic character, Arthur Fonzerelli, AKA the Fonz, epitomized coolness with his leather jacket, ladies' man charm, and popularity. Yet, his inability to apologize or admit fault was one of the Fonz's notable flaws. In numerous episodes, the Fonz would try to admit he was wrong, but when he tried to say the actual words, it would always come out as gibberish, humorously portraying his struggle to own up to mistakes.

We all encounter moments in life where we falter, disappoint others, or misspeak. I've personally stumbled in professional scenarios, friendships, and family interactions, owning up to countless instances where I've missed the mark. Knowing I messed up, I'd stew on the matter, and the situation would only get bigger and bigger in my mind, making the apology more difficult to provide.

As flawed beings, we must accept that we are destined to sin and hurt others, leading to disappointments in human connections and disappointing our Creator as well.

But there is an easy remedy—the freedom of apology!

Acknowledging our fallibility is the first step to progress. Admitting our mistakes, asking for forgiveness, whether from others or confessing our wrongs to God, becomes a pivotal release from the weight of guilt. While an apology doesn't erase the past, it signifies remorse, a commitment to repair relationships, and a resolve to grow from these experiences.

The power of a genuine apology is transformative. It liberates us from the shackles of guilt, allowing us to embrace a sense of freedom and restoration. On the flip side, avoiding apologies leads to resentment, an urge to rationalize our own missteps, and an accumulation of unresolved emotions that can magnify minor issues over time. From personal experience, I can tell you that holding onto an apology that needs to be given is never the right approach.

Ultimately, the choice between liberation and confinement often rests in acknowledging the potency of an apology. It's an essential part of accepting responsibility, fostering growth, and nurturing healthier relationships, granting us the freedom to move forward with grace.

> **Quotable:** "Apologizing does not always mean you're wrong and the other person is right. It just means you value your relationship more than your ego" (Mark Matthews).

> **What does scripture say?** "Therefore, let's keep on pursuing those things that bring peace and that lead to building up one another" (Romans 14:19).

Reflection: Who is someone in your life that you need to apologize to? Pray that God will give you the courage to take that step.

Take time to reflect on your notes from last week. What worked and what didn't?

_____

_____

_____

_____

_____

What is one goal I want to be intentional about accomplishing this week?

_____

_____

_____

_____

_____

What is one relationship I am going to focus on this week?

_____

_____

_____

_____

What is one thing I can do this week to better my physical and/or mental health?

_____

_____

_____

_____

_____

What am I grateful for in my life right now?

_____

_____

_____

_____

Spend time in prayer following the P.A.T.H. (Praise, Admit, Thank, Help).

YOU®

THE BRAND OF YOU

U pon graduating from college in 2000, the vast majority of my private sector career was spent in the marketing and advertising world. During that time, I witnessed the ebb and flow of various marketing trends, all subject to the evolving whims and preferences of consumers.

Amid this dynamic advertising landscape, one steadfast truth persisted—the immense influence wielded by building a powerful brand. Put simply, a brand encapsulates the emotions, sentiments, and impressions linked to something. When you hear Montana, your immediate associations craft that state's brand. Similarly, your initial thoughts that come to mind about Nike or Ronald Reagan instantly conjure the respective brands they have built.

When looking at the brands of individuals, I've discerned that exceptional leaders distinguish themselves by deliberately shaping their personal brands. Everything from attire choices to the content shared on social media, the language they use, and their treatment of others—these elements, amongst many others, all play a part in forming one's personal brand.

Just as a single negative encounter with a restaurant or a clothing label can swiftly stain its brand in a consumer's eyes, the same holds true for personal interactions. Constructing a reputation takes a lifetime, yet it can be marred in mere moments. Each daily interaction you engage in serves as a deposit into your personal brand bank account. Are you consistently making substantial, quality contributions to this account? Is your online footprint an accurate portrayal of who you want to be?

Consider how those around you might respond to the question: "When I mention YOUR NAME HERE, what comes to mind?" Aligning your actions with your desired answer to this question should shape your life in a manner that defines your brand accordingly.

A crucial facet of personal branding is its perpetuity—it's a continuous, round-the-clock process. Your brand doesn't toggle between work, church, or social outings on a Friday evening. Being conscious of the perpetual impact you have on those around you, irrespective of the setting, should steer your actions, shaping your identity in accordance with the distinctive life that God has called you—and only you—to lead.

> **Quotable:** "Your brand is what people say about you when you are not in the room" (Jeff Bezos).

> **What does scripture say**? "In the same way, let your light shine before others that they may see your good deeds and glorify your Father in heaven" (Matthew 5:16).

Reflection: When you think about how others may describe you when you are not in the room, are you at peace with your personal brand? If not, what can you do to change it?

Take time to reflect on your notes from last week. What worked and what didn't?

_____

_____

_____

_____

_____

What is one goal I want to be intentional about accomplishing this week?

_____

_____

_____

_____

_____

What is one relationship I am going to focus on this week?

_____

_____

_____

_____

_____

What is one thing I can do this week to better my physical and/or mental health?

_____

_____

_____

_____

_____

What am I grateful for in my life right now?

_____

_____

_____

_____

_____

Spend time in prayer following the P.A.T.H. (Praise, Admit, Thank, Help).

WELL DONE, GOOD AND FAITHFUL SERVANT

Early in my tenure as Mayor of Sioux Falls, I encountered a moment that reshaped how I approached honoring retiring city employees. One day, in my massive stack of items awaiting my signature, was a routine letter for a dedicated employee's retirement after twenty-five years of service. The informality of both the letter and the method of delivery of the well wishes struck me as overly impersonal. That's when I resolved that, for as long as I held office, I would personally meet and acknowledge every retiree, extending a handshake and a heartfelt gift from my office. Little did I anticipate this gesture would encompass over 250 retirees throughout my eight-year tenure!

As I embarked on this commitment, I decided to provide each retiree a small, framed print bearing the words, "Well done, good and faithful servant." This message held a deliberate dual meaning, honoring their service as public servants while also encapsulating a faith-based send-off, drawing inspiration from Matthew 25:23. To this day, these interactions with each retiree remain among my most cherished memories from my time as mayor.

In the renowned parable of the talents in Matthew 25, we uncover a profound lesson about embracing our role in God's kingdom. Two servants, entrusted with significant gifts, display trust in their master by investing these gifts. However, the third servant, lacking trust, fails to invest and faces loss—of both the gift and his employment—upon the master's return.

Consider the notion of facing our Maker someday, having our life assessed, and hearing those words, "Well done, good and faithful servant." There's hardly a sweeter affirmation! Each day presents an opportunity to audit our words, thoughts, and deeds, ensuring we maximize the gifts bestowed upon us in service to the kingdom. Our daily aspiration should be to live in a way that one day, we receive those profound words from our Lord. What a day that will be!

> **Quotable:** "God continually tests people's character, faith, obedience, love, integrity and loyalty" (Rick Warren).

> **What does scripture say?** "Whoever keeps his commandments abides in God, and God in him. And by this we know that he abides in us, by the Spirit whom he has given us" (1 John 3:24).

> **Reflection:** Are you willing to risk earthly comforts in order to do the will of the Lord in your life?

Take time to reflect on your notes from last week. What worked and what didn't?

_____

_____

_____

_____

_____

What is one goal I want to be intentional about accomplishing this week?

_____

_____

_____

_____

_____

What is one relationship I am going to focus on this week?

_____

_____

_____

_____

_____

What is one thing I can do this week to better my physical and/or mental health?

_____

_____

_____

_____

_____

What am I grateful for in my life right now?

_____

_____

_____

_____

Spend time in prayer following the P.A.T.H. (Praise, Admit, Thank, Help).

WEEK 47

THE "US" IN CONSENSUS

When reflecting on exceptional leaders you've encountered, certain common traits often surface. Among the myriad qualities that define strong leadership, one pivotal trait stands out as indispensable—the ability to forge consensus.

Over the years, I've had the privilege of collaborating with remarkable individuals and witnessing high-level executives, community leaders, and politicians in action. While their styles and approaches vary greatly, the hallmark of their success lies in their ability to rally people toward a shared objective or cause.

Allow me to illustrate the significance of consensus-building through an experience during my tenure as mayor. Faced with a decision concerning an aging and decaying community building, I overlooked seeking community input, disregarding the sentimental attachment many residents held toward this relic. Despite what I believed was a clear and obvious decision I needed to make, a segment of the community vehemently disagreed, sparking a need to halt and reconvene stakeholders. This instance underscored the importance of involving others in decisions, even seemingly straightforward ones, and forced me to reassess the assumptions I was making.

Consensus-building doesn't entail abandoning our beliefs or values. Instead, it navigates the natural tensions inherent in relationships. Whether it's a marriage, friendship, or any human interaction, our self-interests often clash. Yet, fostering consensus involves honoring diverse perspectives and forging mutually agreeable solutions without compromising personal convictions.

There's wisdom in the adage that a leader without followers is merely taking a walk. In essence, effective leadership, whether in the workplace, home, or community, hinges on the ability to inspire others to join in the journey. True leadership involves not just charting a path but also engaging and inspiring others to walk alongside in pursuit of a common destination.

> **Quotable:** "No doubt, unity is something to be desired, to be striven for, but it cannot be willed by mere declarations" (Theodore Bikel).

> **What does scripture say?** "I will instruct you and teach you in the way which you should go; I will counsel you with My eye upon you. Do not be as the horse or as the mule which have no understanding, whose trappings include bit and bridle to hold them in check, otherwise they will not come near to you" (Psalms 32:8-9).

> **Reflection:** Is it possible to build consensus while not compromising your beliefs and values? Where is God calling you to lead more boldly in your life?

Take time to reflect on your notes from last week. What worked and what didn't?

_____

_____

_____

_____

_____

What is one goal I want to be intentional about accomplishing this week?

_____

_____

_____

_____

_____

What is one relationship I am going to focus on this week?

_____

_____

_____

_____

_____

_____

What is one thing I can do this week to better my physical and/or mental health?

_____

_____

_____

_____

_____

What am I grateful for in my life right now?

_____

_____

_____

_____

Spend time in prayer following the P.A.T.H. (Praise, Admit, Thank, Help).

GIVING QUIETLY
OR OUT LOUD?

During my time as mayor, one of the most gratifying aspects was witnessing the remarkable financial generosity of our community in supporting various city projects. From parks, pools, and bike trails to museums and military initiatives, there were always community members ready to step up when a crucial need arose.

This culture of generosity was not just for city projects but extended to our non-profit sector as well. Rarely did a capital campaign or charitable drive fall short of its financial target. Often, the impetus for this success came from significant donors whose contributions encouraged others to join in. Giving tended to spark more giving, a cycle I witnessed time and again within our community.

There's a nuanced perspective when it comes to public recognition of donations. My family has contributed to causes that have been publicly acknowledged, admittedly providing a sense of satisfaction. Yet, there have also been instances where our contributions remained anonymous, silently impacting projects without receiving any acknowledgment—an equally fulfilling experience.

Public recognition holds importance in inspiring others to engage with, and support causes they might otherwise overlook. Personally, my family has been motivated to support initiatives by observing others' generosity, fostering a desire to contribute to something larger than we could ever accomplish on our own.

Yet, there are moments when adhering to Jesus' counsel is essential: "But when you give to the needy, do not let your left hand know what your right hand is doing, so that your giving may be in secret. Then your Father, who sees what is done in secret, will reward you" (Matthew 6:3-4).

God doesn't seek our money but desires our hearts. He perceives the intent behind each donation—whether it's for public recognition or a quiet, faithful act of stewardship. Sometimes, our giving serves to inspire others, while at other times, it's about quietly serving God by sharing His blessings with others. As long as our intentions are sincere, each gift brings joy to our Father.

> **Quotable:** "Christian giving is to be marked by self-sacrifice and self-forgetfulness, not by self-congratulation" (John Stott).

> **What does scripture say?** "Each of you should give what you have decided in your heart to give, not reluctantly or under compulsion, for God loves a cheerful giver" (2 Corinthians 9:7).

Reflection: Being honest with yourself, do you give so that others can see, or do you give in obedience to God? If you are not a faithful giver, what small steps can you take to form a habit of giving?

Take time to reflect on your notes from last week. What worked and what didn't?

_____

_____

_____

_____

_____

What is one goal I want to be intentional about accomplishing this week?

_____

_____

_____

_____

_____

What is one relationship I am going to focus on this week?

_____

_____

_____

_____

_____

What is one thing I can do this week to better my physical and/or mental health?

_____

_____

_____

_____

_____

What am I grateful for in my life right now?

_____

_____

_____

_____

_____

Spend time in prayer following the P.A.T.H. (Praise, Admit, Thank, Help).

WHAT DO YOU DO?

Our careers often play a significant role in defining who we are and where we find our identity. Think of names like Jeff Bezos, Tom Brady, or Teddy Roosevelt, and our immediate association links them to their professional endeavors—entrepreneurship, football, politics. Given that a substantial portion of our waking hours is devoted to work, it's natural for our identity to intertwine closely with our careers.

I firmly believe God encourages us to take great pride in our work, using our talents to excel in our professions. After all, one of the first directives God gave to man in Genesis 2 was to "work the Garden of Eden and keep it." However, there's a danger when we tether our primary identity solely to our career. Careers, like all things in life, have finite trajectories. Layoffs, career changes, retirements—they are all opportunities for an identity crisis if our work is where that primary identity is found. Placing our core identity in our job title or current occupation places it in an impermanent and unpredictable realm.

I've witnessed the struggle many face when involuntary job loss or retirement prompts a search for self-definition. Who am I without my career identity? It's a challenge many of us have faced or will face in the future. While our work remains a part of who we are, our fundamental identity should rest in our relationship with Christ, recognizing ourselves as children of God. Understanding this truth provides a steadfast anchor, assuring us of our place in this world regardless of the unpredictable course our careers may take.

Imagine the next time you're introduced at an event, and the customary question arises, "What do you do?" Consider responding, "I'm a child of God, and I work as a _____." Doing so will emphasize that you know where your primary identity resides and that your earthly career, while important, is second to who you are in Christ.

> **Quotable:** "If anything becomes more fundamental than God to your happiness, meaning of life, and identity then it is an idol" (Timothy Keller).

> **What does scripture say?** "Before I formed you in the womb I knew you, before you were born I set you apart; I appointed you as a prophet to the nations" (Jeremiah 1:5).

> **Reflection:** When considering your identity, do you place too much emphasis on your career? What can you do to remind yourself regularly that your true identity is only found in Christ?

Take time to reflect on your notes from last week. What worked and what didn't?

_____

_____

_____

_____

_____

What is one goal I want to be intentional about accomplishing this week?

_____

_____

_____

_____

_____

What is one relationship I am going to focus on this week?

_____

_____

_____

_____

_____

What is one thing I can do this week to better my physical and/or mental health?

_____

_____

_____

_____

_____

What am I grateful for in my life right now?

_____

_____

_____

_____

_____

Spend time in prayer following the P.A.T.H. (Praise, Admit, Thank, Help).

TO STAND OUT, STEP UP

I n the realm of work, the hunger to distinguish oneself is always present. We work extra hours, meticulously curate our social media presence, dress for impact, and ensure our projects catch our boss's eye, all in a bid to ensure our hard work doesn't go unnoticed. The ultimate aim? Recognition for our efforts—a bump in pay, a step up the career ladder, or perhaps a brand-new career opportunity spotted by someone noticing and acknowledging our efforts.

I've long held the belief that the most standout individuals are those who tackle the tasks nobody else desires or, oftentimes, even thinks about. The truly remarkable people I've worked with in my career are those who consistently, positively, and selflessly handle the small, seemingly easy tasks with excellence.

If you aim to make an indelible impression at your workplace, here are some simple yet impactful actions bound to catch everyone's attention:

1. Consistently arrive not just on time, but five minutes early, for every commitment, meeting, and obligation.
2. Exude positivity—be the beacon of cheerfulness in the room, uplifting those around you without being overbearing.
3. Employ positive body language: lean in when others speak, avoid distractions like checking your phone, and actively listen to those sharing.
4. Cultivate a reputation as the go-to person for going the extra mile, lending a hand, and consistently surpassing expectations.
5. Maintain an insatiable curiosity—ask questions, seek knowledge, and absorb the invaluable wisdom from those who have been at your work longer than you.

The beauty? None of these actions hinge on a specific job title or placement on the organizational chart. The potential to stand out and be recognized is within your grasp, waiting for you to seize it. So, go ahead—embrace these qualities, start doing the small things with excellence, and make your mark.

> **Quotable:** "It's the little details that are vital. Little things make big things happen" (John Wooden).

> **What does scripture say?** "He will bless those who fear the Lord, both the small and the great" (Psalm 115:13).

> **Reflection:** Are you frustrated with your career trajectory in some way? Step back and ask yourself if you are doing the small things well and trusting God in the process.

Take time to reflect on your notes from last week. What worked and what didn't?

_____

_____

_____

_____

_____

What is one goal I want to be intentional about accomplishing this week?

_____

_____

_____

_____

_____

What is one relationship I am going to focus on this week?

_____

_____

_____

_____

_____

What is one thing I can do this week to better my physical and/or mental health?

_____

_____

_____

_____

_____

What am I grateful for in my life right now?

_____

_____

_____

_____

_____

Spend time in prayer following the P.A.T.H. (Praise, Admit, Thank, Help).

WEEK 51

CARING FOR THE POOR

've always felt uneasy using the term "poor" to label individuals. In our society, it often brings to mind an image of someone lacking material possessions—a home, a car, adequate clothing, or financial stability. No one desires to be categorized as "poor," and certainly, no one actively pursues a life defined by poverty.

During my tenure as mayor, one pressing issue that drew considerable attention was homelessness. It stands as one of the most visible manifestations of poverty in our communities, and it often elicits compassionate responses from those compelled to aid the homeless. I have personally always felt a calling to care for those experiencing homelessness, but in a way that properly balances compassion with self-motivation.

In one poignant moment from Jesus' ministry, while enjoying a meal in the town of Bethany, a woman anointed his feet with expensive perfume, prompting some to criticize the apparent extravagance of the act. They suggested selling the perfume and using the proceeds to assist the poor. Jesus responded, "The poor you will always have with you, and you can help them any time you want. But you will not always have me" (Mark 14:7). His statement, "The poor you will always have with you," highlights the enduring nature of poverty, homelessness, and financial hardship in our world.

However, this doesn't imply turning a blind eye to those in need or accepting poverty as an inescapable reality. Instead, God presents an opportunity through the plight of the poor—to exhibit compassion, empathy, and care for the marginalized, which is exactly what Christ did during his earthly ministry. That calling to care for the poor is something each and every person of faith should not quickly dismiss. If you lack financial resources, offer your time; if time is limited, extend your influence. As Romans 12 emphasizes, "We have different gifts, according to the grace given to each of us." While poverty persists, our response, following Christ's example, should embody caring for those in need, as Scripture very clearly teaches us.

> **Quotable:** "Good works is giving to the poor and the helpless, but divine works is showing them their worth to the One who matters" (Criss Jami).

> **What does scripture say?** "Since there will never cease to be some in need on the earth, I therefore command you, 'Open your hand to the poor and needy neighbor in your land'" (Deuteronomy 15:11).

> **Reflection:** Being honest with yourself, how would you grade your work in helping the poor in your own community? Do you view this as someone else's work, or are there ways you can be more active in this work?

PAUL TENHAKEN

Take time to reflect on your notes from last week. What worked and what didn't?

_____

_____

_____

_____

_____

What is one goal I want to be intentional about accomplishing this week?

_____

_____

_____

_____

_____

What is one relationship I am going to focus on this week?

_____

_____

_____

_____

_____

What is one thing I can do this week to better my physical and/or mental health?

_____

_____

_____

_____

_____

What am I grateful for in my life right now?

_____

_____

_____

_____

_____

Spend time in prayer following the P.A.T.H. (Praise, Admit, Thank, Help).

WEEK 52

BURSTING YOUR BUBBLE

We reside in an era where information access is unprecedentedly abundant. While traditional media like television, radio, and newspapers once dominated our media landscape, they now contend with social media, emails, text messages, news apps, and an array of digital platforms. This surge in avenues for information consumption should ideally foster a more informed populace. However, a significant portion of the content disseminated through these channels is saturated with half-truths, misinformation, and bias-confirming narratives.

I ventured into Twitter's early days in 2007, back when only the true "digital nerds" were on board. Today, it stands as a primary news source for many, including the media. Within the realm of social media, we often follow like-minded individuals and pages, engage with brands that align with our preferences, and absorb content from politically skewed news outlets that reinforce our existing viewpoints. This pattern cements our perspectives, making them more rigid, biased, and entrenched.

Similar dynamics manifest in our relationship circles. We naturally gravitate toward individuals who resemble us—be it in demographics, spirituality, politics, or other facets. This tendency perpetuates our online echo chambers, reflecting themselves in our real-life interactions.

My role as a mayor compelled me to engage with individuals whom, outside of my position, I might never have encountered. It has necessitated challenging conversations, demanding more than a Facebook meme to defend beliefs and immersing me in environments that prompted deep reflection on my convictions. Stepping beyond my comfort zone into relationships and scenarios that challenge my identity has underscored the rarity of absolute truth and underscored the paramount importance of an open-minded approach to contemporary issues.

Embrace the discomfort that comes from hard discussions—dare to burst your bubble, engage in diverse circles, and converse with individuals from vastly different walks of life. Through this experience, you will realize that life is not as black and white as it may seem and discover that with many in our world, we are much more alike than unalike.

> **Quotable:** "It is never too late to give up your prejudices" (Henry David Thoreau).

> **What does scripture say?** "Do nothing out of selfish ambition or vain conceit. Rather, in humility value others above yourselves, not looking to your own interests but each of you to the interests of the others" (Philippians 2:3-4).

Reflection: Thinking about your own media consumption and relationship circles, how open are you to listening to the opinions and views of others? What can you do to become more open-minded to various topics of the day?

Take time to reflect on your notes from last week. What worked and what didn't?

_____

_____

_____

_____

_____

What is one goal I want to be intentional about accomplishing this week?

_____

_____

_____

_____

_____

What is one relationship I am going to focus on this week?

_____

_____

_____

_____

_____

What is one thing I can do this week to better my physical and/or
mental health?

_____

_____

_____

_____

_____

What am I grateful for in my life right now?

_____

_____

_____

_____

_____

Spend time in prayer following the P.A.T.H. (Praise, Admit, Thank,
Help).

Quarter Four Check-in

Congratulations on following *The Code of Contentment* for the year! Take time now to look back over your journaling from the entire past twelve months. When you've finished doing that, review the following questions:

How did I do with the goals I set this past year? Where did I succeed, where did I fail, and what have I learned about myself in this process?

_____

_____

_____

_____

_____

_____

What have been my biggest wins with the relationships I have focused on? What relationships do I need to continue to improve?

_____

_____

_____

_____

_____

Being honest with myself, how do I feel about my physical and mental health right now? Have I made an impact on my overall wellness this past year?

_____

_____

_____

_____

_____

Thinking about my last year, what areas of my life am I most thankful for?

_____

_____

_____

_____

_____

SO, NOW WHAT?

My hope is that if you're reading this, you've triumphantly completed the fifty-two-week journey through *The Code of Contentment*. You've diligently set goals, uncovered newfound gratitude for life's blessings, fostered your physical and mental wellness, grown in your walk with God, and enriched vital relationships along this path. Congratulations are in order!

So, what lies ahead?

Now, it's about progression. It's time to solidify and amplify the habits you've nurtured over this transformative year.

Maintain a steady, unwavering rhythm for prayer and devotion, exploring resources that deepen your journey. When prayer feels uncertain, remember the P.A.T.H. (Praise, Admit, Thank, Help)—a reliable starting point.

Seek ways to augment the investments in your physical and mental health, striving for gradual yet significant enhancements.

Never underestimate the power of gratitude; it's a lens revealing blessings when you pause to acknowledge them.

Craft goals, both lofty aspirations and small, achievable milestones, and steadfastly follow your plans to conquer them. Remember, a goal without a plan is just a wish.

Life isn't a destination; it's an ongoing voyage. Each day offers a chance to refine ourselves and draw closer to the embrace of our Heavenly Father.

Once again, congrats on taking a year to invest in yourself. Now, go out and take that bold next step, leaning into your faith through the concepts you've worked on through this book and continuing to crack the code of contentment!